CW00329304

A ROYAL
LOVE
devotional

....

100 MOMENTS
WITH *The* KING

CORRINE SHARPE

♥

Published by Sharpehouse
www.corrinesharpe.com
csharpehouse@gmail.com

Library of Congress Control Number: 2020917855
ISBN: 978-0-578-71327-4

Heart Photography by Corrine Sharpe and multiple contributors with written consent
Editorial by Kimberly Smith Ashley, The Editor Garden info@editorgarden.com
Book Layout by Summer Morris, Sumo Design Studio
Cover photo by istock.com

Printed in the United States of America

DEDICATION

This book is dedicated to my beautiful family and my friends who are like family. To my husband, Erik, you are my biggest encourager, and without your love and support, I would not be who I am today. To our children, Hayden and Loren, you bless me and give me so much strength as I watch you serve the Lord with all your hearts. To my mother-in-law, Kathy, who is a second mom to me, your love and grace is a gift to our family.

And I will give them a heart to know me, that I am the Lord; and they shall be my people, and I will be their God: for they shall return unto me with their whole heart.

JEREMIAH 24:7 KJV

♥

INTRODUCTION

God uses all of creation to draw us to Himself. One of the ways God uses His creation—for me and many others—has been through the image of hearts, in many different creative forms, and through God's providential timing to convey His love and presence. The heart photos and encounters in this devotional are moments with the King. Every day our King walks with us and talks with us. In these daily moments, we encounter pure love and truth from our Heavenly Father so that we may be healed and made whole. For each person that is led to read this devotional, I pray you are reminded or made aware of how much God loves you and is for you. While reading each day, take a pause and ask God to reveal His heart to you. In every moment with the King, our God pours out His love and gives us our identity and value as His daughters. Healing doesn't happen by might or power of man, but by the Spirit of the Lord. Systems made by man for spiritual growth are good, but they will not make us whole. It is encountering Jesus' pure love that breaks statistics and generational bondages and that heals our soul wounds.

The hearts are just one example of how God's grace and love reaches out to minister to His people. My first book, *A Royal Love Revealed: My Journey from Sorrow to God's Heart*, written after losing my mother to breast cancer, followed

God's heart story of taking me and others from sorrow to joy. God would reveal hearts to me and my family in the most perfect timing and creative ways. Since the first book, the heart story has reached people around the world and many others in my circle of influence. God does not have favorites. I am free and whole because I have a relationship with Jesus. If I would have denied the power and love of Jesus, I probably wouldn't be here today. The world will tell us who we are and what we will become based on our life circumstances. But God came for redemption for all people and to give us hope and a future through the supernatural ways of our Creator.

God told me that this heart story was for anyone who will receive it. No matter what circumstances we face, God wants us to know that He is with us and is working on our behalf to give us a future and a hope. Each of us has an important, original part to play in the story of redemption and of helping others find their first love, Jesus. We are made in the image of Christ, for a specific time and place, to be His image bearers. There is a seat at the Lord's table for everyone, and God's resources are endless and supernatural for healing every heart. When we learn how much we are loved by God and encounter His consuming love, we may extend that same love to those around us. But we first need to look in the mirror and allow God to speak His truths to our own hearts and reveal our true selves so that we may align with heaven.

The hearts from God are so gracious. They help us to focus on Him and receive His love and word, which gives us lasting joy and peace. When we aren't just focused on ourselves and our own circumstances, we let the Lord lead, and we yield to His presence for His purposes in our lives. He is able to fix our thoughts because our thoughts are fixed on Him. We learn to trust Him because we are connected to Jesus, our source of life.

Through a relationship with Jesus, we are able to learn the Father's ways and fulfill the plans He spoke over us before we were in our mothers' wombs.

When we receive Christ and His glory into our hearts, we are adopted sons and daughters and become a part of an eternal kingdom. We receive a supernatural and limitless inheritance from our Creator that is given to us through Jesus. Each of us was created out of love, to be loved by God. We must stay the course of heaven and dwell in God's perfect peace to be able to receive God's royal love that makes us whole, healed, and free to love. All glory and honor to our King.

CHOSEN
VESSELS

Let each of you look not only to his own interests,
but also to the interests of others.

PHILIPPIANS 2:4 ESV

God knows what we need and when we need it. I know we don't always like to hear that. The hearts are a symbol of practicing listening, seeing and hearing the prompts of the Holy Spirit. When we yield to God's plans and allow interruption in our daily lives it creates a space for the Holy Spirit to move and breathe through His chosen vessels. The Lord chose us as His family before the foundations of the earth.

God wants us to show his love in ways that meet the deep needs of others around us that only He knows. My mother in law had multiple love notes on her birthday given to her through her granddaughter, Loren's eyes. The above heart photo happened while we were celebrating at lunch. It was unexpected and most importantly Loren was willing to be interrupted. "Pay careful attention to yourselves and to all the flock, in which the Holy Spirit has made you overseers, to care for the church of God, which he obtained with his own blood." Acts 20:28 ESV

PRAYER

Heavenly Father, help me to see the needs of others around me. Manifest to me how to allow interruption in my daily plans to show love and care to those around me. Thank you for the honor of serving Your people that you laid Your life down for. In Jesus' name, amen.

BEING KNIT TOGETHER IN LOVE

That their hearts may be encouraged, being knit together in love,
to reach all the riches of full assurance of understanding and the
knowledge of God's mystery, which is Christ. In whom are hidden
all the treasures of wisdom and knowledge.

COLOSSIANS 2:2-3 ESV

The road to God's love is magnificent and full of surprises. Our
stories are frequently being intertwined as the children of God.
He wants us to be in His family. And the Lord desires for each
of us as children of God to be family to one another. We have a
desire for a healthy community and family because He set that
on our hearts. When we are growing our spirit in Jesus' truths,
it is then that we will be able to love others as ourselves.

At every turn He has something just for you and a benefit for sharing it with others. God is drawing each of us to Himself and His story. His love reaches as far as the north from the south and as far as the east is to the west. This photo was captured on the freeway in California as the sun was coming up on a new day of possibilities.

PRAYER

Father, I want to see Your love around me and share Your love with others so that we can all be knit together in Your love. Soften my heart to see the value in others and the value I have in You. I thank you that a cord of three strands is not easily broken. In Jesus' name, amen.

UNSPEAKABLE
JOY

May the God of hope fill you with all joy and peace in believing,
so that by the power of the Holy Spirit you may abound in hope.
ROMANS 15:13 ESV

We have unspeakable joy through hearing and believing the truth of God's word. When we believe God's word and speak it over dark circumstances, we experience unspeakable joy. This kind of joy can only come from the Holy Spirit. God gave us the Holy Spirit to make us whole and give us all of His attributes, which transcends our world's systems and expectations. God's peace and hope gives us our strength. Though we have not seen

Him, we love Him, and though we do not see Him now, but believe in Him, we experience great joy!

I spotted this heart on my daily walk, as I was praying that God give me His joy for my sadness in a dark circumstance that I was going through. No matter how dark of a place you may find yourself, there is always hope in Jesus to bring you out and to the other side. He alone is our hope and joy. The Holy Spirit wants to walk through these dark times with us and guide us to higher ground, where He continues to grow us to be more like Him.

PRAYER

Thank You, Father, that when I run to You first and ask for Your peace and joy to fill my heart, you do so generously. I ask You, Jesus, to help me to turn my gaze and focus on You and Your love, no matter what I am facing. I know that when I put my trust in You that You will turn all of my sadness and despair into great joy because of Your great love for me. In Jesus' name, amen.

SEEING GOD WITH OUR MINDS AND HEARTS

Whoever has my commandments and keeps them, he it is who loves me. And he who loves me will be loved by my Father, and I will love him and manifest myself to him.

JOHN 14:21 ESV

When we commit ourselves to Jesus' ways and commands, He manifests Himself clearly within our minds. He has so much love to give and show us each day. These hearts are just one example of God's mercy and grace to draw our eyes up to Him and on His presence. Jesus knows how hard this fallen Eden is to endure. Living by our Savior's commands isn't just about following His rules; it's a way of living so that our minds may receive His workings, wisdom, and presence.

DAY
4

It is miraculous how the Lord works through our subconscious and our conscious. When we keep His commandments, they save us from emotional strongholds and entanglements of the heart that draw us away from our Father. We learn how to follow our Heavenly Father's patterns, and not the world's, which enables us to be led in a relationship by Him and His sacred plans He has set apart for us. He knows the way to open the door for each one of us to encounter and know the overflowing love of the Holy Spirit.

PRAYER

Heavenly Father, give me eyes to see Your presence in my life. Help me to focus my mind on You and Your ways so that I may see the greater purpose of having a relationship with You. Let it be as Your word says, that whoever keeps His word, truly the love of God is perfected in him. By this, I know I am living for the Lord. In Jesus' name, amen.

THROUGH GOD
WE WILL DO
VALIANTLY

Oh, grant us help against the foe, for vain is
the salvation of man! With God we shall do valiantly;
it is he who will tread down our foes.

PSALMS 60:11-12 ESV

Have you ever been in a situation where you feel like there is no help from anyone? And, in that moment, you think everything is hopeless, and you feel lost, and you can't go on? Today, I want to encourage you that when we learn to listen and receive from Jesus' word, we will hear strength, hope, and love. When we release our trust to our Heavenly Father, He will take care of our enemies and trials. Man is not our savior, but God is.

In the book of Psalms, we are encouraged by God's truth. The word is God and is alive and active, moving on our behalf supernaturally. We shall go boldly and courageously because of Jesus. If you are like me, you don't always feel bold or courageous. But if we know and trust the living God, He will provide us with these attributes to give us the determination and the ability to be overcomers, no matter what we face.

PRAYER

Heavenly Father, I am grateful for Your love and courage You give me in the hardest moments of my life. It is by Your strength and courage that I may go boldly into the unknown and overcome the attacks against me. You alone make the fearful bold by the power of Your Holy Spirit. I ask You to guide me in trusting You with every challenge I face so that You may always show me the way of escape. In Jesus' name, amen.

A MOTHER'S
LOVE

And his mother treasured up all
these things in her heart.

A mother's love or a mother figure can be a powerful influence in the hearts of their children. I am thankful for a mom who loved the Lord and taught me the importance of having a relationship with Jesus and keeping my worth in Him. Perfection isn't the goal. Rather, a relationship with Jesus is the goal. The overflow from that relationship is where the supernatural happens, and we are changed from the inside out forever. Once we know Jesus, it doesn't matter where we come from or what we have been told our whole lives. He will restore every part of us to whom He made us to be.

The grace and love that flows from Jesus into our hearts is what enables us to be healthy, giving individuals for the ones that we mother. Studies have shown that the strongest influences on children's lives are their parents. If we want to change the world, it has to start at home. This heart photo and moment with King Jesus was on Mother's Day. The Lord was so gracious to show me and another friend, whose mom is in heaven, these hearts in nature. It was a reminder to me of the importance of continuing to teach my children about Jesus' love and faithfulness. We are reminded in Proverbs that the wisdom of God will be life to our souls and grace to our necks.

PRAYER

Heavenly Father, help me to have words of graciousness and life to reach the children's hearts I speak into. Guide me in Your ways so that I may be a reflection of Your heart for Your children. Give me understanding in how to yield to Your word and let my words be Yours, no matter what circumstances I face in mothering those around me. Thank You for the honor and privilege to speak Your truths into Your children. In Jesus' name, amen.

KNOW THE
VOICE
OF TRUTH

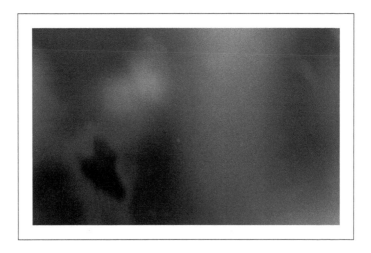

May my teaching drop as the rain,
my speech distill as the dew, like gentle rain upon
the tender grass, and like showers upon the herb.

DEUTERONOMY 32:2 ESV

How many voices do we listen to each day? How often do we listen to the voice of the enemy? The enemy wants to pull us as far away from God and who He made us to be as often as possible. The authority above all of these voices is Jesus' voice. His voice is always kind, loving, and uplifting, and speaks honor and value to His people. He doesn't talk to one person more than another; however, it is our choice to create space and set aside time to hear from the Lord. In Proverbs 2, we

DAY 7

are encouraged to receive the Lord's words and treasure up His commandments, making our ears attentive to wisdom and inclining our hearts to understanding.

It is up to each of us to receive His commandments and to live by them so that our hearts aren't clouded or closed off with sin and hardness. When our hearts are soft to the things of God, we are open to being attentive to His wisdom within His voice and His word. We can also know when we hear His voice because it always agrees with the word of God. Most important, our hearts are able to store away in their chambers the mysteries of the Holy Spirit and understanding His ways.

PRAYER

Heavenly Father, no matter what happens, I know I can come before You. Your voice is like a gentle rain upon the tender grass. Your love never ends. Open my eyes to understand the power and love of Your voice. Let me hear Your voice so that it guides and protects me in Your perfect love. Help me to know Your voice of truth and to quiet all else so that I may receive Your wisdom. In Jesus' name, amen.

OUR GOD IS IMMENSE AND YET INTIMATE

O Lord, you have searched me and known me! You know
when I sit down and when I rise up; you discern my thoughts
from afar. You search out my path and my lying down and are
acquainted with all my ways. Even before a word is on my tongue,
behold, O Lord, you know it altogether. You hem me in, behind
and before, and you lay your hand upon me.

PSALM 139: 1-5 ESV

When we look at His creation, we see how immense our God
is. How He formed the wide oceans and vast mountains, and
how all that is living on the land lives in perfect harmony.
Also, when we have any type of health issue, we get a
glimpse of how intricate and complex our bodies are, and
how miraculously they function every day. Our God is both
immense and intimate in His creation. The Trinity gives us

the most perfect example of how perfect intimacy works. We are to follow God's blueprint in the Trinity.

God's love for us is in the details. In Zephaniah 3:17, the word tells us that God rejoices over us; He both quiets us with His love and exults over us with loud singing. Our God sees every detail of our lives, and not only sings over us, but also loudly sings over us. We can see His intimate love for us in the details of scripture. God hems or surrounds us from behind and before and lays His hand upon us. Our God holds us together, and He finds us all together lovely in who we are becoming. When we come to know this, His love guides us in how we are to treat and let ourselves be treated by others we have intimacy with on earth.

PRAYER

Father, search my heart and show me Your ways on how to be intimate with You and the people You bring into my life. Remove those relationships that are not from You. Strengthen me to walk in Your ways of intimacy and trust Your higher ways. In Jesus' name, amen.

MY DAYS WERE FORMED BEFORE I WAS IN MY MOTHER'S WOMB

For you formed my inward parts; you knitted me together in my mother's womb. I praise you, for I am fearfully and wonderfully made. Wonderful are your works; my soul knows it very well. My frame was not hidden from you, when I was being made in secret, intricately woven in the depths of the earth. Your eyes saw my unformed substance; in your book were written, every one of them, the days that were formed for me, when as yet there was none of them.

PSALM 139: 13-16 ESV

The heart shells in the photo above were found by me, my daughter, and her friend that came to visit for my daughter's birthday. The single, most powerful thing that we can learn as women—young and old—is, as it is written in Psalm 139, that our substance and significance was seen by God before we

were formed into a person and a solid presence. God wrote out our days before we ever had a day on earth.

We have been wonderfully made in the depths of the earth, fully seen by God. He gave us His purposes to live out on this earth before we were in our mother's wombs. This should compel us to know our Heavenly Father and the plans He has for us. These plans are what give us life, and give us life more abundantly, of far more than we can dream or ask. No matter what imperfect family structure we were born into, this is our heritage. Our value, identity, and heritage come from the Lord.

PRAYER

Heavenly Father, Your word says that You saw me in my unformed state and knit me together in my mother's womb. I am fearfully and wonderfully made by You. Your thoughts for me are precious and outnumber the grains of sand. Search my heart and remove any thoughts that aren't from You. Lead me in Your everlasting ways. In Jesus' name, amen.

GOD'S STRENGTH AND LAWS IMPRINTED ON OUR HEARTS

I will put my laws into their minds, and write them on their
hearts, and I will be their God, and they shall be my people.

HEBREWS 8:10 ESV

Through His grace, God imprints and writes His laws on our
minds and hearts so that we understand them through the
new covenant. In the new covenant, we have a relationship
with Jesus. He doesn't hide His wisdom from us or His ways.
He makes everything known to us in plain sight so that we do
not have any confusion.

The heart in the photo above appeared on my sister-in-
law's, Cheryl's, door. An imprint of the Father's love for His

daughter. The signs and wonders that the Holy Spirit did in the book of Acts through His apostles are still being written today through His daughters. We are adopted daughters the moment we receive Jesus into our hearts. It was by God's strength, through Moses, that He led His people out of Egypt, and it is by God's strength that He will lead us out of the Egypt that is in our hearts.

PRAYER

Dear Heavenly Father, I am so thankful for Your strength that You give so freely. For when I am weak, You are strong. Thank You that You lead me out of dark circumstances through the truths that You have graciously imprinted on my heart and mind. Help me to open my heart to Your covenant and the truths You have for me. In Jesus' name, amen.

GOD'S MERCIES ARE NEW EVERY MORNING

The steadfast love of the Lord never ceases; his mercies never come to an end; they are new every morning; great is your faithfulness. "The Lord is my portion," says my soul, "therefore I will hope in him." The Lord is good to those who wait for him, to the soul who seeks him. It is good that one should wait quietly for the salvation of the Lord.

LAMENTATIONS 3:22-26 ESV

We are encouraged to not fret over evildoers that prosper in their ways. Fretting only causes harm to us, both physically and emotionally, and makes us more stressed than when we started. The Lord tells us to cease from anger and wrath. Psalm 37 shares with us that our Lord fights for us, that the wicked will be cut off, and that those of us that seek and wait on Him shall inherit the earth. He says, too, that we will delight

ourselves in an abundance of peace when we put our hope in Him, wait quietly, and delight in our Savior.

Through our commitment, He gives us the desires of our hearts and His overflowing mercy. Whatever circumstance we wake up to for the day, we may trust He is with us in the waiting and is working all things together for our good. The Lord's provisions and blessings are always worth the wait because they are always beyond what we could ever dream or imagine. How encouraging it is that we have God's forgiveness and love every morning.

PRAYER

Heavenly Father, my heart takes courage in knowing that You are with me in every step of every day. Thank You for Your never-ending mercies. You are my portion, and Your steadfast love fills my heart with everlasting hope. In Jesus' name, amen.

LIFE FOUND FROM OLD GROUND

Set your minds on things that are above, not on things
that are on earth. For you have died, and your life is hidden
with Christ in God. When Christ who is your life appears,
then you also will appear with him in glory.

COLOSSIANS 3:2-4 ESV

God calls us to put on our new self when we become Christ
followers. He tells us to put our minds on the things of His
kingdom, not on the world we live in daily. There is power and
peace in turning away from the earthly passions of immorality,
impurity, jealousy, and idolatry. In our western world, we are
surrounded by these desires, temptations, and choices. We are
called to put these things away when we follow Jesus. God

knows that we can't have a new self while continuing to carry this baggage with us.

We put on our new selves by learning His living word and growing in the knowledge of our Creator's ways. We may find abundant life in Christ in the middle of a chaotic world because we are made in the image of Christ, and Christ is all and in all things. In Christ, hope is found through our old ground. There is no shame in growing from our old selves to a new place of wholeness in Christ. The intentional choices we make clear the path for us to walk as children of the light and to be a beacon for a miraculous God.

PRAYER

Heavenly Father, You defeated the darkness of this world and gave me new life. As I learn Your ways, I want to put them into practice in my life. I am grateful that my old ground can spring forth a new life, as I set my mind on You and reflect on who You are. I give You all the glory and honor. In Jesus' name, amen.

DELIVERED
FROM TROUBLES

When the righteous cry for help, the Lord hears and delivers
them out of all of their troubles. The Lord is near to the
brokenhearted and saves the crushed in spirit.

PSALM 34:17-18 ESV

Jesus experienced everything that we experience in our lives.
He is not far off and disconnected from His people. He is
with us and intervenes on our behalf daily. The above photo
was from a friend whose MRI results had been cleared for a
health issue. Our vision needs to be clear and our hearts pure
in seeking the Lord. Psalm 34 also says that when we seek
him, He hears us and saves us.

DAY
13

The angel of the Lord encamps around those that fear Him and He delivers them. This fear is reverential, full of trust in God's ways and provision. We must ask ourselves if we are following His righteous ways. Our obedience to His ways builds us up in righteousness. The Lord says that His eyes are on the righteous, and when they cry out, He will deliver them from all of their troubles. The power and love in these scriptures saves our spirits and holds us together in His perfect love, no matter what we are facing.

PRAYER

Heavenly Father, You deliver me from my troubles daily. I may rest assured knowing that Your timing is always perfect. Help me to live in righteousness and choose Your word first in every situation I face. Thank You for Your supernatural power that lives and breathes into my life daily. In Jesus' name, amen.

WE ARE THE
APPLE OF HIS EYE

For thus said the Lord of hosts, after his glory
sent me to the nations who plundered you, for he who
touches you touches the apple of his eye.

ZECHARIAH 2:8 ESV

My sister, Alecia, saw this heart on the apple at the grocery
store, as she was calling on the Lord for direction and help for
things going on in her life. The Holy Spirit sees our pain and
concern, and gives His love to the deep places of our hearts.
He so generously gives us vision for the moment, in every step
we take, to keep us moving forward.

Proverbs 7 further explains that the Lord compels us to keep His commandments and to keep His teaching as the apple of our eyes. What a beautiful exchange we see, here in scripture, of us being the apple of the Lord's eye, and each of us, in return, keeping His commandments and teaching as the apple of our eyes. Our Creator wants us to dwell in the land with Him. He is not ashamed of us and calls us into a relationship with Him daily. We were made to be His chosen family.

PRAYER

Heavenly Father, Your love for me shines bright through Your word. Your words are sweet and soothing to my soul. Help me to receive the revelation of Your love for me. Your love is without blemish. Your love is pure and holy. Your love is what my heart longs for. Thank You that when I seek You, I will find You. I am made whole in Your love. In Jesus' name, amen.

COMPLETE LOVE

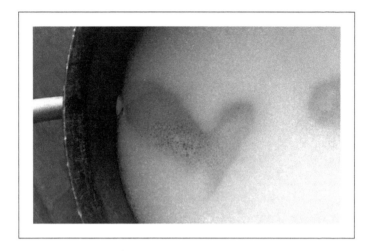

And above all these put on love, which binds
everything together in perfect harmony. And let the
peace of Christ rule in your hearts, to which indeed you
were called in one body. And be thankful.

COLOSSIANS 3:14-15 ESV

A friend saw this heart after her friend had told her about receiving some difficult news and was asking for prayer. Moments like these help us to understand that we are the Lord's beloved. We learn that we are never alone and that if we go to the Father and pray first that He will give us His attributes of tender mercies, kindness, humility, meekness, and longsuffering in the midst of the challenges we may be

facing. As sisters in Christ, we are called to bear one another's burdens and to pray for one another.

The word shows us the way to dwell with Christ and how to give the Lord praise through our actions and deeds. Women both young and old have the ability to connect so quickly and be transparent with one another. This is a gift from God, and it is to be valued and celebrated, not used to create division or compete against one another. When we live out our relationships God's way, He sharpens us and brings harmony to our lives in a world of indifference.

PRAYER

Thank You, Father, that You give me the best example of relationship in the Trinity. Help me to see the gift in inviting Your peace to rule in my heart. I can love others well when I know how much I am loved by You. Thank You for Your love and the gift of friendship and wholeness. In Jesus' name, amen.

HEIRS OF GOD

But when the fullness of time had come, God sent forth his Son, born of woman, born under the law, to redeem those who were under the law, so that we might receive adoption as sons [and daughters]. And because you are sons, God has sent the Spirit of his Son into our hearts, crying, "Abba! Father!" So you are no longer a slave, but a son, and if a son, then an heir through God.

GALATIANS 4:4-7 ESV

The heart photo on this page was taken on Father's Day. A sweet reminder of who our Father is for eternity. We are born into all different kinds of families, and we experience great joy and great pain in those families. Regardless of the wellbeing of our earthly families, we can have the parent that we know our heart needs through a relationship with Jesus. The Lord gave

up His life so that we may give up ours, to dwell with Him and be His daughters.

When the Holy Spirit enters our hearts, we become His adopted children and are heirs to the Lord. The King of Kings, the Lord over all Lords! We may trust that our hearts are being laid in our Heavenly Father's hands. He will breathe life, healing, peace, wholeness, purpose, hope, love, worth, forgiveness, and all the many mysteries of His kingdom into our hearts. We are children of God, and He is our good Father.

PRAYER

Heavenly Father, it is so comforting to know that I am Your daughter. Help me to frame my decisions and my heart around my inheritance in You. You are a good Father, who works all things together for my good. Help me to learn about my inheritance in You. There is no better place to be than at home with You in my heart. In Jesus' name, amen.

CROWNED WITH LOVE
AND COMPASSION

Bless the Lord, O my soul, and forget not all his
benefits, who forgives all your iniquity, who heals all your
diseases, who redeems your life from the pit, who crowns you
with steadfast love and mercy, who satisfies you with good
so that your youth is renewed like the eagle's.
PSALM 103:2-5. ESV

This is my niece, Mia, who was crowned on her eighth birthday
by her Heavenly Father's love and compassion. Mia was born
with multiple heart defects and has had many heart surgeries
since her birth. She is an overcomer, and her God has renewed
her youth and blessed her soul. The Holy Spirit has endless
ways that He wants to bless us and encourage us. He lovingly
displays His righteous, loving hand over our lives.

DAY
17

We can put our hope in the Lord, for in Him is mercy and abundant redemption. When we have a relationship with God first in our lives, He redeems us from all of our iniquities. We may be satisfied in all the good He provides for us. It's not a coincidence either that, in the Bible, the number eight is a symbol for resurrection and regeneration. It denotes a new beginning and man's true, born-again event. When our Father talks to us and guides us through our hardest, most unsure times, there are often so many layers and depths to His love, which He expresses to His daughters to bring them healing.

PRAYER

Heavenly Father, You bless my soul. Your encouragement and kindness know no end. You are my merciful Father, and You crown me with Your steadfast love and mercy. Thank You for satisfying me with Your goodness and forgiveness. In Jesus' name, amen.

GOD'S MASTERPIECE

For we are his workmanship, created in Christ
Jesus for good works, which God prepared beforehand,
that we should walk in them.

EPHESIANS 2:10 ESV

This heart photo was a sweet reminder to my daughter's best
friend that God chose her first. You, His daughters, are His
masterpiece. In Ephesians 2, the Lord tells us that we were
created for Him, and according to His good pleasure that by
His grace, we are accepted as His beloved. God's grace is what
enables us to be strong, to choose to stand on our faith, and to

DAY
18

remain loyal. God placed our value on us when He formed us in the secret place.

It is by grace that we are saved by faith. A masterpiece is an original, invaluable work. That is how God sees you, before you ever do anything good. God gives us the gift of grace through the blood of Jesus so that we may draw near to Him. Daughter, you are God's masterpiece, and your Father made plans for you as citizens from heaven and members of His household.

PRAYER

Father, guide me to the plans that You have made for me. I know that Your plans are the best plans and that You will give me Your peace as I trust in You. Strengthen my faith, and give me more of Your wisdom and knowledge to walk in. Thank You for revealing more of Your love and my heritage to me. In Jesus' name, amen.

OUR HEARTS
HAVE A REFUGE

For you have been my help, and in the shadow
of your wings I will sing for joy. My soul clings to you;
your right hand upholds me.

PSALM 63:7-8 ESV

What is better than life? What could possibly fill us more than just living? Jesus Himself. If we have lived long enough, many of us have been through some battles. Battles and hard places make us brittle, dry, weary, and empty. In the shadow and strength of our loving Father's arms, the Holy Spirit quenches our thirst with His goodness. It is here, in His presence, that

we see His loving-kindness is better than life. And our hearts may cling to all of His glory and faithfulness and give us wings again to flourish.

When we take the time to be with our Father, we are able to receive His supernatural ways of refreshing us and comforting us in refuge. The book of Psalms says that He commands His loving-kindness in the daytime to us, and that in the night, His song shall be with us. We get to experience inexplicable joy, which holds us up to more than just living. We are made aware of the God of our lives and the refuge we attain beneath His wing.

PRAYER

Father, thank You for Your loving-kindness and for Your right hand that holds me up. It is a blessing to know that my strength and help come from the Lord. How beautiful to know that my Heavenly Father puts a song over me at night. Lord, You are my exceeding joy. In Jesus' name, amen.

OUR REST

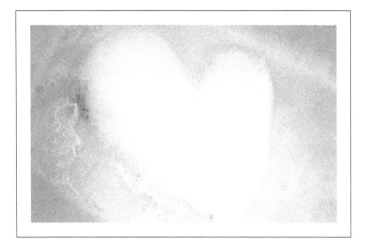

Come to me, all who labor and are heavy laden, and I will give
you rest. Take my yoke upon you, and learn from me, for I am
gentle and lowly in heart, and you will find rest for your souls.
For my yoke is easy, and my burden is light.

MATTHEW 11:28-30 ESV

The heart photo above was a sweet gift from our Father to
Kimberly, my editor. Just when we think we can't go on is
when we receive this beautiful invitation of rest for our souls.
Once again, we are made aware of this exchange with our
Father in our souls when we seek Him, choose Him, and take
Him at His word. Our Father sees us in our current states.
He is neither a task master, nor is He interested in showing

us all of our faults. Instead, He extends an invitation for us to experience a humble and gentle Father that gives us rest and makes our burdens light.

He gives us eternal life and a fulfilling life here on earth. Jesus gives life to all the things that are burdensome, here and now. He says all that come to me shall not hunger and all who believe shall not thirst. The words our King speaks to His daughters are spirit and life. They revive and sustain us in our souls.

PRAYER

Father, You revive my soul and call me to a place of rest, no matter what circumstances I am in. Your presence is full of joy and rest for Your daughters. Help me to remember that when I am burdened, I am to run to Your presence first and receive Your words of life. Quiet my heart so that I may learn Your ways and have a yoke of lightness. Thank You for Your sacrifice of breaking Your flesh so that mine may be made whole. In Jesus' name, amen.

ETERNAL ROOTS GROWING IN OUR HEARTS

That according to the riches of his glory he may grant you to be
strengthened with power through his Spirit in your inner being, so
that Christ may dwell in your hearts through faith—that you, being
rooted and grounded in love, may have strength to comprehend
with all the saints what is the breadth and length and height and
depth, and to know the love of Christ that surpasses knowledge,
that you may be filled with all the fullness of God.

EPHESIANS 3:16-19 ESV

May God's peace, love, and joy increase in our hearts and grow
deep roots. Roots deep into the places of our hearts that need
Him so desperately. First Corinthians shares that no eye has
seen, nor ear heard, nor has anyone entered into the heart of
man the things that God has prepared for those who love Him.
This is for every daughter. Scripture teaches us that God has

revealed these things to us through His Spirit, and that His Spirit searches all things, including the deep things of God.

The fullness of God being revealed to us through the Holy Spirit, to our inner spirits, is the only way that we may have the strength to comprehend the all-consuming powerful love He has for His daughters. Our flesh is too weak and doesn't have the capability to understand the fullness of God. Our answers are found in a relationship with Jesus, not in how we can be like someone else. Each daughter is His pride and joy. In His fullness, Jesus fills us all, and at His table, there is a seat for everyone.

PRAYER

Heavenly Father, open the eyes of my understanding so that I may fully receive the sacred eternal love You have for me. I love You with all that I am, and I thank You for accepting me just as I am. Thank You for making me whole through the power of Your Holy Spirit. I give You all the honor and praise. In Jesus' name, amen.

LOVE NEVER FAILS

Love is patient and kind; love does not envy or boast; it is
not arrogant or rude. It does not insist on its own way; it is not
irritable or resentful; it does not rejoice at wrongdoing, but rejoices
with the truth. Love bears all things, believes all things, hopes all
things, endures all things. Love never ends.

1 CORINTHIANS 13:4-8 ESV

The type of love that never fails is the love that comes from
our spirit, and not from our flesh. It's not birthed out of our
passions, but is birthed through Jesus and given by God.
God is love. The attributes of love as described in scripture
can only be attained through a relationship with Jesus. First
Corinthians says that if we have all the faith, knowledge, and
gifts from the Spirit but do not have love, then we are like a

clanging cymbal and are nothing. I am sure some of us know people that have these gifts, but they do not have love. It changes our perception of God, sometimes, but it shouldn't.

People are not God. It is up to us, as His daughters, to grow in our love with Him and our love toward others. No one is complete, apart from our Savior. We are all moving at different time frames toward Him. Jesus draws us all to Himself. We want our words to be words that heal and build up those around us so that our sound is pleasant. Love never ends, because God never ends. First Corinthians also instructs us to have three things: faith, hope, and love. And the greatest of these is love.

PRAYER

Father, Your word says that love is the greatest thing we need to fix our hearts on You. Build up within me the attributes of Your love. Holy Spirit, fill me so generously with more of You, as I surrender to Your ways of showing love. Thank You that Your love flows freely through me. In Jesus' name, amen.

BLESSING OF RETURNING TO GOD

And the Lord your God will circumcise your heart and the
heart of your offspring, so that you will love the Lord your God
with all your heart and with all your soul, that you may live....
And you shall again obey the voice of the Lord and keep all his
commandments that I command you today.

DEUTERONOMY 30:6, 8 ESV

We are so overwhelmed in our luxurious culture with how to
look and act, and we are encouraged to focus on ourselves. For
women and girls, the images on social media platforms send
the wrong messages. We can quickly be sent into dark places
that cause us to think, *I'm not enough* and *I need the validation
of my peers in order to feel valued.* Chasing these things will
never bring us peace, wholeness, or value. If anything, we
become more stubborn in our own ways. The scripture in

Deuteronomy shows us how to live. How to live above all of the distractions and to bring God's full blessings and honor into our lives.

Jesus wants to write His love on our hearts and fulfill every area of our hearts and life, as we show our loyalty to Him. Through a relationship with the Holy Spirit, He circumcises our hearts. We don't hide our sin, but confess it. We are reminded of our covenant with Him by keeping our souls in His truth and light. Deuteronomy 10 tells us that through circumcising our hearts that we will no longer be stubborn. When we are dedicated to keeping the commandments of our King and humbling our hearts to receive His truths, we will be free to truly live in the favor and protection of our covenant with Him.

PRAYER

Heavenly Father, I surrender to Your ways. I will keep Your commandments by following Your voice. Awaken my soul to Your many benefits and love that You have for me. Thank You for blessing the generations after me through my obedience. In Jesus' name, amen.

BEAUTIFUL ONE

You are altogether beautiful,
my love; there is no flaw in you.
SONG OF SOLOMON 4:7 ESV

I feel like, as girls, we are so quick to point out our flaws. As if we need to bring ourselves down to relate and feel accepted. I also think that this is our response, sometimes, due to what our culture or families may project onto us. There is this unspoken standard, and outside of that, everything else doesn't measure up in what is beautiful. I am so thankful that this is not the kingdom's truth. Our Creator made each one of us perfectly and without flaw.

He is a perfect God and makes everyone beautiful. Beauty truly comes from within and radiates from our hearts. Our standard of beauty needs to come from our Heavenly Father. It changes how we see our own value and the value in others. When we place His value and beauty on every person we meet, we see them as God sees them. God created His people out of love and for love. Our call is to return to our first love, to see the beauty in ourselves and His people. Song of Solomon 2:4 teaches us, "And his banner over me was love."

PRAYER

Father, You alone set Your love upon me and give me value and beauty. I am lovely and flawless in Your sight. Your love reaches to every part of my soul and gives me life. Thank You for Your consuming love that is my strength. I will gladly serve You all the days of my life. I am grateful for the way You love me. In Jesus' name, amen.

OUR HEAVENLY FATHER AND BEING EQUALLY YOKED

I will make my dwelling among them and walk among
them, and I will be their God, and they shall be my people.
Therefore go out from their midst, and be separate from
them, says the Lord, and touch no unclean thing; then I will
welcome you, and I will be a father to you, and you shall be sons
and daughters to me, says the Lord Almighty.

2 CORINTHIANS 6:16-18 ESV

This heart photo encourages and calls us into faith with
Jesus. Our Father dwells with us and walks with us. He calls
us to step away from being unequally yoked together with
unbelievers. Second Corinthians and Romans 8 instructs us
that righteousness should not fellowship with lawlessness and
questions us about what communion has light with darkness.

We are to lead by righteousness (which is our spirit), and not follow our flesh. This kind of fellowship is unstable in all of its ways. By letting our flesh lead us, we experience confusion and strife.

As daughters of the King, we may live a peaceful life if we are spiritually minded. When we become believers, we are set free of the bondages of fear and instability. We may call on our Father as heirs of God, and everything that we suffer here may be glorified. There is no glory, only death, to all hope, faith, and love when we are ruled by our flesh. The same Spirit that raised Jesus from the dead is alive in His children and that same Spirit is what gives us an abundant life.

PRAYER

Heavenly Father, thank You for Your Holy Spirit who helps me in my weaknesses. I am an adopted daughter and heir with Christ. Empower me to walk as a child in the light. Reveal to me how to be led by the Holy Spirit in all I do for Your kingdom here on earth. I give You all of the honor and glory! In Jesus' name, amen.

A ROYAL
PRIESTHOOD

But you are a chosen race, a royal priesthood,
a holy nation, a people for his own possession, that you
may proclaim the excellencies of him who called you
out of darkness into his marvelous light. Once you were not a
people, but now you are God's people; once you had not
received mercy, but now you have received mercy.

1 PETER 2:9-10 ESV

You are chosen and precious to our Heavenly Father. In First
Peter, the Lord is telling us that we are a holy people, and
therefore we should act like it. We are to put away malice,
deceit, hypocrisy, envy, and slander. I am sure we can think of
times in our everyday circles of life where we experience these

types of behaviors, or, sometimes, when we are tempted to respond in these ways. But our Lord says to put them away.

We have God's mercy, so let's act like it and turn from these entanglements. We may be rejected by people because of it, but it's okay because we are a part of something much greater. Because we are chosen and precious to God, we are being built up as a spiritual house of living stones. We are a royal priesthood who offer our sacrifices to our Father. In exchange, we are not put to shame but have honor in our lives and an inheritance in heaven, which is an imperishable seed.

PRAYER

Father, thank You for Your grace and mercy in my life. I come to You with thanksgiving for the imperishable seed You have given me. It is an honor to be rejected by man for Your sake and to be given everything for all of eternity. Guide me in Your grace every day so that I may be a light and beacon of who You are. In Jesus' name, amen.

WALKING THROUGH IT IN JESUS' LOVE

And because lawlessness will be increased, the love
of many will grow cold. But the one who endures to the
end will be saved. And this gospel of the kingdom will be
proclaimed throughout the whole world as a testimony to
all nations, and then the end will come.

MATTHEW 24:12-14 ESV

We go through a lot of brokenness in our lives. We live in
a world of broken systems. And we are all broken, to some
extent, in our souls. It is too easy to respond in anger and
hatred. But Jesus came to redeem each one of our hearts and
souls so that we may, in His love, walk through it and show
others the way.

If we will turn to Jesus in those times of anger and hurt, and receive His portion of love and grace, we can be filled up and healed. Then, we may respond how He would have us respond, and we may be made whole. In Ezekiel 36, God says He gives us a heart of flesh for our hearts of stone. It all begins with the heart, if we will surrender it to the One who created it. God sustains us by Himself, as He is our bread of life. Our source of wholeness doesn't come from an apology; it comes from our King.

PRAYER

Father, I know the only one who can give me love to make me whole is You. Your love is pure fire to my soul. It ignites healing and belonging in such an intimate and personal way. I walk away changed and in awe of Your wonder and grace. Guide me to You when I feel angry and hurt, because I know it is only in Your presence that I will be made free and be who You have called me to be. In Jesus' name, amen.

OUR HEAVENLY FATHER
IS OUR ANCHOR

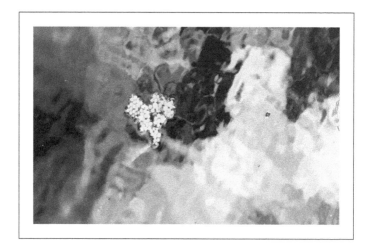

We have this as a sure and steadfast anchor of the soul,
a hope that enters into the inner place behind the curtain, where
Jesus has gone as a forerunner on our behalf, having become a high
priest forever after the order of Melchizedek.

HEBREWS 6:19-20 ESV

Jesus, our High Priest, came and gave up His life to fulfill the law. His sacrifice is for everyone and for all of time. The veil kept us from approaching God in the Old Testament, but now, in the New Testament, a new covenant has been established so that you, His daughters, can approach Him

through a relationship. Hebrews also teaches us that we are priests forever and have an endless life.

Death has lost its sting. Our King's priesthood is for eternity. He has saved us completely and forever and will always make intercessions for His people. We are not tossed from circumstance to circumstance. Instead, we stand firm, as if tied to an anchor, through the circumstance. We have this anchor and this hope in Jesus, who is perfecting us forever. We receive the Lord's promises and become conquerors, as He sustains us in every storm through His word and His royal priesthood.

PRAYER

Heavenly Father, I have hope, as Your priest, that You are my anchor for my soul. You bring hope in my storms. Your promises are sure and steadfast to those who love You. I put my hope and trust in You in the storms of my life. I am sustained in Your presence and renewed by Your intercessions. Lead me to Your promises when I am weak. In Jesus' name, amen.

TRUSTING
IN GOD

You have kept count of my tossings; put my
tears in your bottle. Are they not in your book?

PSALM 56:8 ESV

This I know, God is for us. I was making a meal for a family
that lost a loved one due to cancer. As I was preparing their
dinner, I prayed for them, and God showed up. I saw this
sweet potato in the shape of a heart. God carries our sorrows
for us and gives us hope. This psalm is saying that He sees us,
comforts us, remembers us, and loves us.

One day, He will wipe away every tear, and death will be no more (Revelation 21:4). We won't always know why things happen the way they do now, but we may be comforted by His love and know that our trust in Christ will get us through. When we trust our Heavenly Father, He will bring more fulfillment than we could ever imagine on this side of heaven. Ultimately, He will keep us from falling so that we may accomplish all that God has planned for us in preparation for all we will do in heaven.

PRAYER

Thank you, Father, for Your love that keeps count of my tears. You shepherd my heart and keep me in all Your ways. Because of Jesus, You know my losses and pains that bring me sorrow. Show me the way to Your love, which restores my soul, until the day that every one of my tears are wiped away and we are together for eternity. In Jesus' name, amen.

I AM
WITH YOU

The righteous flourish like the palm tree and grow
like a cedar in Lebanon. They are planted in the house of
the Lord; they flourish in the courts of our God.

PSALM 92:12-13 ESV

The love of our Father has no end. Before we ever do one good deed, He loves us. We are fully seen by Jesus and He says, *I love you.* You are never alone, and the love of God continues to pursue each of us. This is endless love. To know our first love enables us to truly love and live. This photo is an example of His consuming, incredible love for my sweet, beautiful sister, Alecia, who has stood on God's promises. She has turned to Jesus for her strength through a few years of the hardest

challenges in her life. She has kept a beautiful heart, in spite of multiple attacks against her.

This is how we stand in righteousness and love. The Father used all the things around her to say, *I'm with you, I love you, lean in and listen to my words and my plans.* They are to prosper you and help you. The cedar, known for its strength against decay, was used in the temples of the Bible. It is a reminder for us that every good gift is from God. We may flourish in His courts because of His gifts that are planted in His spiritual house.

PRAYER

Father, remind me that every good gift comes from You. When I flourish, remind me not to focus on the gift, but to thank You for it and worship You for Your goodness toward me. Guide my heart toward gratitude and keep me far from judgment. In Jesus' name, amen.

LIFE THROUGH
DEAD THINGS

And have put on the new self, which is being
renewed in knowledge after the image of its creator.
COLOSSIANS 3:10 ESV

When we make space to get to know our Creator each day,
He brings life through the dead things in our lives. The things
that are passing by or have had their season in our lives aren't
lost, as He is weaving a deeper story of making all things new
in our hearts. Restoring, maturing, and leading us on a path of
strength and character. We might ask, *why do I need a new self?*
We are born of flesh, and the attributes of flesh lead to death.
When we are born again, we receive a new self and the Holy
Spirit's presence, which leads to life.

DAY
31

The Holy Spirit is now dwelling in us. In our response to being given eternal life and the ability to live by the Spirit, we graciously make the choice to put on our new self and feed our faith through the Holy Spirit in us. When we are adopted as daughters into our God's royal priesthood, we should be loyal to our King's ways. It is exciting to see the changes and healing in our hearts and lives, as we are being renewed and guided to new places of wholeness by our Father in heaven.

PRAYER

Heavenly Father, I live on Your words daily. They feed my soul and mind, and shepherd my heart to peaceful places of rest. Your voice is always kind and gentle, even while being firm. You push me out of my comfort zones so that I may learn to have more trust and reliance on You. You are a safe place, and I put my faith in You as I am renewed each day to Your patterns. In Jesus' name, amen.

BEING ASTOUNDED
IN GOD'S WONDER

"Look among the nations, and see; wonder and
be astounded. For I am doing a work in your days
that you would not believe if told."

HABAKKUK 1:5 ESV

This is the God of love that we get to serve, know, and love. This photo is from a friend who was in A Royal Love Study Group. God brought the wonder of the hearts to her sister before she'd ever heard God's heart story and after her beautiful child went to eternity from brain cancer in 2015. Six

months later, she adopted this dog that had a heart on it. The family didn't notice it until they got home.

Fast forward to 2017, when she learned of God's wonder of the hearts. At the same time, this mother had a heart-shaped leaf on a new bloom in her daughter's remembrance garden. God sees our pain, and His love and mercy reaches beyond our understanding. He moves before, after, and during a miracle. There are so many layers to His goodness and love that we cannot perceive it all. Our omnipresent, omniscient God pours out His wonder and love at all times for the benefit of His daughters and people.

PRAYER

Father, help me to see Your love in my life. Holy Spirit, show me Your goodness when I cannot see. I cannot begin to understand Your ways, but I can find comfort in Your love for me. You fill my cup, even when I feel like I am lost and beyond repair. Your wonder is life to my flesh and heart. You are everything I need until my loved ones and I are all together again in heaven with You. In Jesus' name, amen.

THE LORD'S STEADFAST LOVE

The earth, O Lord, is full of your steadfast
love; teach me your statutes!

PSALM 119:64 ESV

Jesus is always for us and He loves truth and justice. The earth is full of the goodness of the Lord. The Holy Spirit will never disappoint or leave us. He has endless ways to love us, so personally and so perfectly. He moves through the seen and the unseen. The earth is filled with the Lord's love. Sometimes we just look for it in the wrong places.

The Lord works through His ways to benefit us, while also looking at all of time at once. His statutes guide us in His truths so that we may see His goodness and plans. His commandments give us wisdom that surpasses our enemies and raises us up to higher ground for victory in every area of our lives. The King of the universe loves us so much that He would give us all of His benefits. When we gain this understanding of our Lord, it keeps our path lit and strengthens us not to depart from it.

PRAYER

Heavenly Father, thank You for Your steadfast love. Help me to see the things that You want me to do and give me the strength to turn away from the things that are not of You. Your word is a lamp unto my feet and a light to my path. You order my footsteps each day to the places You want me to go. In Jesus' name, amen.

HOW TO WIN
BATTLES

Finally, be strong in the Lord and in the strength of
his might. Put on the whole armor of God, that you may be
able to stand against the schemes of the devil.
EPHESIANS 6:10-11 ESV

Ephesians 6:14-18 shows us how to defend ourselves and who
our battles are really against. The spiritual principalities at
work on this earth are our real battles. Yes, they work through
people. But we may also learn who to take aim at and how to
win the battle. When I read this scripture as a child, I thought
more about the physical aspects of armor and how it is a great
analogy. However, as I grew up, and have applied it and used
this scripture in prayer, I have started to see the power in it,

how God moves on behalf of His people supernaturally for peace and victory.

Our obedience to following His lead on each of these pieces of armor is critical to our ability to overcome spiritual battles. God's strength and power are our sure-fire way to overcome the attacks on our hearts. The heart photo above was on the door of a family we adopted for Christmas years ago. The grandmother that lived there had a profound testimony she shared with us about keeping on the armor of God through trials. The mystery of the gospel, when it is shared for the receiver, is astounding, as well as what it provides to the giver. God's peace and love within faith rests on us all.

PRAYER

Father, I thank You for the victory in all of the attacks against me, which were overcome through my obedience in keeping Your commands. Help me to speak boldly in my prayers and align with Your living words. I want to be sincere and steadfast in making the decision to put on Your armor You generously give each day. I give You all the honor and glory. In Jesus' name, amen.

OPENING OUR EYES
TO GOD'S POWER

They said to him, "We have only five loaves here
and two fish." . . . And taking the five loaves and the two fish,
he looked up to heaven and said a blessing . . . And they all ate
and were satisfied. And they took up twelve baskets full of the
broken pieces left over. And those who ate were about five
thousand men, besides women and children.

MATTHEW 14:17, 19-21 ESV

If you need a miracle in your life, give God room to work
in ways that you would never imagine or expect. God knows
our needs before we say anything. Our miracles are often
delivered in ways that God knows we need. God sometimes
uses unexpected things to open our eyes to His power. In
this scripture, His disciples tell Him to send the people away

because they need to go and eat. Jesus uses this moment to show them a miracle by feeding 5,000 people with only five loaves of bread and two fish.

How much more do we think God wants to show us, through His power and miracles, in our own lives? God is still writing stories through His disciples. Every day, He calls to each of His daughters to represent His kingdom and encounter His mercy and love. My friend Sheila traveled to Israel and stood in the place where Jesus performed this miracle. It was there that she saw these heart stepping-stones in the photo above. God gave her a miracle that day and a reminder of His power and presence.

PRAYER

Father, open my eyes to receive the miracles You have for me. Help me to understand that You know what I need and that Your ways are always better. I am thankful for the power of the Holy Spirit. I ask You to come and dwell with me and show me Your great miracles in my life. I will share the goodness of who You are for all of my days. In Jesus' name, amen.

OUR
SHEPHERD

The Lord is my shepherd; I shall not want.
He makes me lie down in green pastures. He leads me
beside still waters. He restores my soul. He leads me in paths
of righteousness for his name's sake.

PSALM 23:1-3 ESV

It is so profound that no matter what fear we may face that God makes provisions for us. He tells us to focus on faith, rather than our fear, and He will lead us to his table that He has prepared for us. Psalm 23 says that He will anoint our heads, and that His goodness and kindness will follow us for all of the days of our lives. When we turn to Him, instead of ourselves, and keep pure hearts and clean hands, we receive blessings and righteousness

from our Lord. The King of Glory enters into our lives through communion and dethrones our flesh.

Jesus' blood and bread through His sacrifice gives us strength and joy to our hearts. We shall not want, no matter what season we are in. I have had many seasons of pruning, but at the same time, God was building me up from within. Our Shepherd restores us and leads us through all seasons. When we partake in communion with God, He takes His daughters to these peaceful, beautiful places in our spirits. We aren't relying on the physical (our sight), but we are walking by faith, which pleases our Shepherd, granting us our King's inheritance as His royal priesthood.

PRAYER

Heavenly Father, thank You for remembering Your covenant with me. You use all of the earth to bless and provide for me. Shepherd my heart to Your presence and guide me to communion. Thank You for all of the benefits of Your kingdom, which brings me to repentance and peace. In Jesus' name, amen.

THE HOLY SPIRIT IS
OUR FRIEND

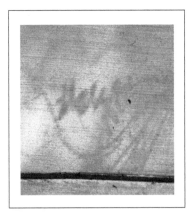

But the Helper, the Holy Spirit, whom the Father will send in my
name, he will teach you all things and bring to your remembrance
all that I have said to you. Peace I leave with you; my peace I give to
you. . . . Let not your hearts be troubled, neither let them be afraid.

JOHN 14:26-27 ESV

The Holy Spirit is the best friend we'll ever have. Scripture
tells us, throughout the book of Romans, how the Holy Spirit
helps us. The Holy Spirit sees us in our weaknesses and gives us
what we need to be strong, to glorify Jesus, and to help fulfill our
purpose in Christ. He teaches us through scripture and others so
that our hearts are changed through community. He shows us the
ways to apply His truths to our lives so that we aren't confused
or lost. The Holy Spirit uses our prayers to change us, and He
intercedes on our behalf in prayer. If we don't understand what to
pray, all we have to do is ask and He will help us.

DAY 37

God's purposes are revealed to us through the Holy Spirit. Oftentimes, we may think that our purposes have to be something of earthly importance or big in the world's eyes. However, our purposes are to glorify God in all we do and to love others how Jesus has loved us. Through doing that first, God works out all of the details in our lives, such as jobs, marriage, and where He wants us planted. Lastly, the Holy Spirit also convicts us of our sins. We need to be made aware of our sins, as His daughters, so that we may become more like Jesus. He helps and guides us in His wisdom. The photo above was from my friend Annie. It was a heart shadow from a tree. Miraculously, within the shadow, she saw the heart and the word love within it. Ultimately, the Holy Spirit is our comforter. He is within us and hovers over us, pouring His love out for all of our days.

PRAYER

Thank You, Father, for the gift of the Holy Spirit. I cannot think of any greater friend. Your love pursues me and keeps me in all Your ways. Guide me to live by Your grace and peace. Teach me to be more like You so that I may be a light for You. In Jesus' name, amen.

WISDOM IN
FRIENDSHIPS

Make no friendship with a man given to anger,
nor go with a wrathful man, lest you learn his ways
and entangle yourself in a snare.

PROVERBS 22:24-25 ESV

We all have imperfections and times when we know we could have done better within our friendships. Forgiveness is so important for ourselves and others, even if we never receive apologies for anger that is directed at us. When we forgive others, it's not letting them off the hook; it's letting ourselves off the hook, from holding offense in our hearts. Bitterness can take root and harden our hearts. Scripture gives us direction on how to guard our hearts and keep us free from unhealthy friendships.

DAY 38

When I discovered the verse above in the Bible, it opened my eyes to the danger of anger. Our Heavenly Father loves His daughters and desires to keep us from things that would ensnare our souls. It is a reminder for us not to have wrath and to not be in close relationship with someone who has anger, because it will be a trap for our souls. An angry man stirs up strife. Living under strife affects every area of your physical health and soul. Fury, wrath, and anger from friends or spouses create fear in those around them. Fear is a tool of the enemy to dismantle the banner of love over each of us. Jesus gave us freedom from oppression and to have peace and life more abundantly so that we may do the will of the Father.

PRAYER

Heavenly Father, I surrender to Your guidance and instruction. Thank You for delivering me from things that would entangle me and pull me away from Your presence and will for my life. Your peace You left to me, and I gladly cling to it and walk in it so that I may live in freedom. I give You all the praise and honor for keeping me in Your peace. In Jesus' name, amen.

PRAY
FIRST

And he told them a parable to the effect that they
ought always to pray and not lose heart.
LUKE 18:1 ESV

Have you ever gotten a phone call that changed your entire day?
You received bad news. Then, to top it off, everything seems to
be crumbling apart. Don't they say that bad things happen in
threes? Not always, but I think, sometimes, we feel the hardships
of life piling up on us. We can quickly begin to feel hopeless and
overwhelmed. May I suggest that you pray first. Even before
calling a friend or family member to discuss it. I have learned, so
many times, that if I stop and pray that it changes my heart and
mind about my circumstances immediately.

God knows what we are facing and has supernatural answers that are far better than what we, or anyone else, can think up as a solution. I know for myself I need Jesus' response, because mine falls short. After losing an earring my mom gave me before she passed away, I stopped and prayed, instead of going into despair. I had to continually pray for a few weeks that God would lead me to the earring. And He was so faithful to do it. I found it where it fell, even though I had vacuumed over that spot multiple times. Keep praying and keep believing while the Lord molds your heart for greater blessings and solutions. Even when things don't turn out the way we want them to, we can trust God's plan.

PRAYER

Heavenly Father, prayer is our lifeline to You and Your ways. Thank You for always answering in Your perfect timing. I believe that I receive what I pray for because Your word is truth. I will pray without ceasing and praise You for all of the hidden wonder You show me through prayer. In Jesus' name, amen.

WHAT WE CULTIVATE WILL GROW

And Isaac sowed in that land and reaped in the
same year a hundredfold. The Lord blessed him.

GENESIS 26:12 ESV

Childlike faith cultivates a pure reliance and trust on Jesus.
Scripture tells us to approach our Heavenly Father in this way.
The Lord knows the way for us to encounter a supernatural,
powerful Creator. We can't have pride in our own knowledge
or have learned behaviors that want to box in the majesty and
power of our Lord. We need to take the time to cultivate a
relationship with Jesus. *Cultivate* means "to care for." What do
we take care of in our lives?

Are we trying to manage our own stress, insecurities, and
anxieties? Are we putting up a daily smoke screen of what

we want others to see? Are we hiding and spreading false narratives so that we can feel better about ourselves? As daughters of a King, we don't need to behave this way. Jesus provided freedom and wholeness on this side of heaven. All we need to do is trust in our Savior and what He speaks over us in His word.

Let's take a moment to think about what we have been cultivating in our lives. Are we holding onto our strong faith and trusting in God's word for us, or are we trying to control all the many worries and stresses in our daily lives? We need to take these pauses and align ourselves with what God provides and cultivates in us when we surrender to His relentless love. We can grow in love for ourselves and each other when we do it God's way.

PRAYER

Thank You, Father, for Your word that is food for us to cultivate our lives for Your people. I want to cultivate a life that reaps all of Your wholeness. Help me to sew Your imperishable fruit and seed in my life. Guide me away from empty pursuits that would bring poverty to friendships, work, and my purpose. In Jesus' name, amen.

JESUS IS THE KING
OF OUR HEARTS

For the Lord God is a sun and shield; the Lord bestows favor and
honor. No good thing does he withhold from those who walk
uprightly. O Lord of hosts, blessed is the one who trusts in you!

PSALM 84:11-12 ESV

Lord, test me and examine my heart and mind. Actively seeking
and living by God's wisdom opens doors that no man can shut.
He will meet us at every corner and intersection of our lives. The
Holy Spirit will confirm His presence and demonstrate His love
for us, as we trust Him and continue to move forward in the plans
that He has for us. He will reveal more and more of Himself as
we set our hearts on Jesus.

Jesus wants to be the King of our hearts. The book of Psalms explains that blessed are those who live by integrity and have high moral standards in every area of their lives. We, as Jesus' daughters, are called to live our lives in this way. It matters what is in our hearts and how we express that in our lives. Jesus sees our hearts and is clear in His word about the amazing benefits and blessings He has for us when we live how He has asked us to live. Deceitful men will try to say there is no way to live above reproach, but I would like to share with you, lovely one, that we can do all things through Christ Jesus who strengthens us!

PRAYER

Heavenly Father, I choose to live with honesty and pureness of heart. Keep my heart soft and gentle toward others. I gladly give honor and respect to others because You so generously give it to me. The beauty of Your grace is that I don't deserve it, but You love me so much that You give it to me with a father's heart. Thank You for blessing me with Your favor. In Jesus' name, amen.

WAITING IN
THE STORMS

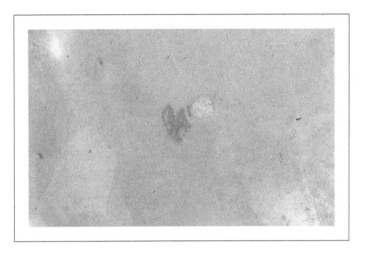

Be strong, and let your heart take courage,
all you who wait for the Lord!
PSALM 31:24 ESV

We put our hope in the Lord when we wait on Him through the storms. His hope does not disappoint. We will not have fear of bad news. We will not be tossed here and there, because we will not be uncertain. Jesus' compassions never fail. Great is His faithfulness! Because of His faithfulness, we may resist the devourer and his ways.

Those who wait on the Lord will be brought to higher ground and established on a strong foundation that does not crumble under pressure. As we practice Jesus' ways, we learn that His word does not return void. Our shield of faith protects us. Our Heavenly Father is loyal to us in His commitment and protection that started with Jesus laying His life down on the cross. His steadfast love covers and restores us as we take courage and walk on the water, putting our hope in Jesus in the storm. He has miracles to show us in the waiting. The photo above was a heart on the ocean floor.

PRAYER

Heavenly Father, I worship You in the waiting. My trust and faith are made strong because I put my eyes and heart on You. You reveal who You are in the waiting and give me courage that I do not have on my own. You have the last say in all things concerning me, and I know Your plans for me come from a well of great love. In Jesus' name, amen.

GRACE
GIRLS

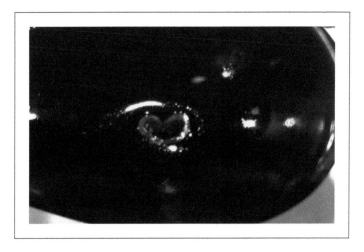

For by grace you have been saved through faith.
And this is not your own doing; it is the gift of God,
not a result of works, so that no one may boast.

EPHESIANS 2:8-9 ESV

Jesus tells us that His grace is sufficient for us and that His power is made perfect in our weaknesses. The strength we have is from His grace, not our own. When we understand that, we may live our lives in humility and peace. First Peter tells us that we should also steward our gift of grace, to faithfully serve in all the ways God asks us to. We should excel toward our sisters and others in being kind, giving, and sharing peace.

Materialism and status in our culture eat away at these principles. They speak the opposite, appealing to our emotions rather than to our humility of focusing on God's truths. Grace girls extend grace and build up those around them. Through knowing Jesus, they see that nothing is withheld from them and they have all they need. Jesus' grace, peace, and value on their lives is what's most important. When we have this knowledge, we can be at peace with our friendships and enjoy the gifts God brings us, without competition and comparison. We can have honor and respect for others, instead of trying to control others because of our own insecurities. None of us can boast, so let's be grace girls.

PRAYER

Heavenly Father, remind me of Your gift of grace You have given to me. Show me how to extend that grace each day to those around me. I need Your grace and truths to guide me through Your word so that I am not led by my emotions. Help me to celebrate the gifts You bring me. Take comparison, the thief of joy, from my heart. In Jesus' name, amen.

GOD'S PROVIDENTIAL ARRANGEMENT OF CIRCUMSTANCES

Now by chance a priest was going down that road,
and when he saw him he passed by on the other side.

LUKE 10:31 ESV

When we think of coincidence, we think of serendipity. A totally random act. But God says that is not so. Of even what seems to us like small or random events, He is in control. The word *coincidence* only appears this one time in scripture, in the book of Luke. And the word *coincidence* is translated in Greek to mean "together with" and "supreme authority." It is so powerful to realize that whatever happens—big or small—occurs because of God's providential arrangement of circumstances.

Proverbs 19 teaches us that the lot is cast into the lap, but that every decision is made from the Lord. Nothing is random and everything is overseen by an omniscient God. The word also tells us that not one bird falls that He doesn't know about. God knows every detail of every hour of our days. God will bring about all of His plans and purposes for all of time. There is nothing unimportant, or too small, to God. He does not grow weary and has limitless power. His attention is never divided, neither is it limited like ours. When sin occurs in our lives, God allows the consequences. However, God also promises to work all things together for the good of those that love Him. He uses our unforeseen events and mistakes to weave His plans and purposes.

PRAYER

Father, You are our Almighty God! You do not grow weary and have no limit to Your power. Help me to see You at work in what I think are unimportant things. Show me the value in having an eternity mindset. Guide me toward experiencing the supernatural moments You have for me so that I may witness Your splendor and share it with others. In Jesus' name, amen.

FULLY KNOWN
AND DEEPLY LOVED

O Lord, you have searched me and known me! You know when I sit
down and when I rise up; you discern my thoughts from afar.

PSALM 139:1-2 ESV

Psalm 139 says that the Lord's thoughts of me are precious and
limitless. He knows every detail of our frames that He created
and knows our ways and thoughts before we say them. I think
we can all agree that we do not always have the best thoughts
and that we do things we regret. Shame wants to keep us in that
place of regret and self-punishment. Our own voices say that no
one can really, fully know us and see our faults, because then they
wouldn't really like us. My friend Christine saw this heart after it
had rained, and the Lord brought the song *Jesus Love Me* to her
memory.

Can we be honest? Everyone on the planet has faults. There is only one perfect person, who is Jesus. If our Heavenly Father can love us first, without us even accepting Him as our Savior, as stated in First John, then we can have His understanding that He sees everything about us and says, *I love you.* God made all of creation for us and for us to enjoy. We were His plan for a family, since the very beginning in Genesis. The Lord will tear down the religious walls and barriers that we have erected as we receive His truth. We are accepted as His beloved. Fully known and deeply loved. This should frame how we think about ourselves and how we extend this truth to those around us.

PRAYER

Father, You made me out of love and for love. I am Your good pleasure, and You have drawn me to You since the day I was born. You show me Your love in Your creation and in moments seen and unseen. You pour Your love into my heart. And You have endless ways that You delight in me. Thank You for Your everlasting love for me. I love You with all that I am. In Jesus' name, amen.

THE ETERNAL KINGDOM

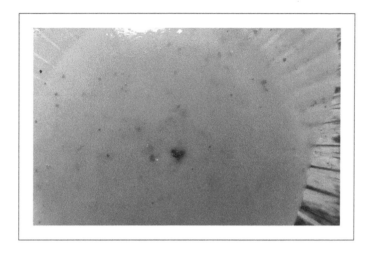

And God, who knows the heart, bore witness to them,
by giving them the Holy Spirit just as he did to us,
and he made no distinction between us and them,
having cleansed their hearts by faith.

ACTS 15:8-9 ESV

This scripture is addressing the Gentiles. We are one family with our Jewish brothers and sisters. The Lord sees all of His people as one family. Romans 10:12-13 teaches us, "For there is no distinction between Jew and Greek; for the same Lord is Lord of all, bestowing his riches on all who call on him. For 'everyone who calls on the name of the Lord will be saved.'" There is one race, which is the human race. Jesus' death and resurrection gave us the new covenant.

The way to God's eternal kingdom is Jesus. John 3:16 says, "For God so loved the world, that he gave his only Son, that whoever believes in him should not perish but have eternal life." We receive heaven when we ask Jesus into our hearts, but we also are called by God to bring heaven's attributes to earth. It is a power and a purpose for here and now. We do not operate under the law of fear any longer, but love. From least to greatest, each one will know the Lord. He writes His laws on our hearts and gives us the ability to understand. We are forgiven of our sins because of the Lamb who was slain for everyone and for all of time.

PRAYER

Father, You are my God and I am Yours. I have life, here and eternally, because I know You. Your love is a consuming fire. I am able to have an eternal mindset and an eternal kingdom because of Jesus' blood. Thank You for a kingdom that cannot be shaken. Shake the things that are not of You out of me so that I may be strong in the things that You placed in me, which cannot be shaken. In Jesus' name, amen.

STEADFAST
LOVE

For your steadfast love is great to the heavens,
your faithfulness to the clouds.
PSALM 57:10 ESV

God's glory is all over the earth. This psalm beautifully describes
that the Lord sends out His steadfast love and faithfulness. The
abuses, loss, and slander that happen to us on this earth by others
will be brought to justice. The ones that create despair for others
will, themselves, be trapped in despair. We are able to praise the
Lord and worship Him through our trials because our hearts are
steadfast on the Lord.

He is so gracious to fill our lives with all of His perfect attributes and hold us together as we trust Him. The heart photo above was confirmation from the Lord after a friend's loved one passed away. There is a reward for the righteous, and all suffering will cease one day. Our hope and trust are in the Lord, and any injustices that we face here on earth will be made right before the Lord. We may see the Lord's faithfulness when we learn about His covering and protection that He extends daily to those that love Him.

PRAYER

Heavenly Father, thank You for Your steadfast love and faithfulness that reach the heavens and clouds. I cannot comprehend the vastness of Your protection and presence in every detail of my life. You never leave me, nor forsake me. And nothing is too hard for You. I am thankful that You redeem every loss and fulfill my days. In Jesus' name, amen.

BLESSINGS
AND CURSES

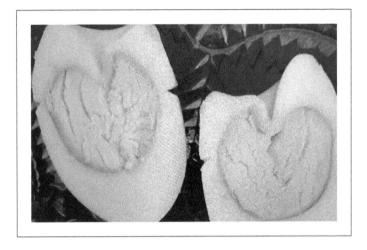

I call heaven and earth to witness against you today,
that I have set before you life and death, blessing and curse.
Therefore choose life, that you and your offspring may live.

DEUTERONOMY 30:19 ESV

We enjoy talking about the blessings in our lives and the ones
that are passed down through our families. We can have a range
of gifts or blessings, whether we are athletic, intellectual, singers,
writers, extroverts, introverts, natural speakers, wise, fearless,
adventurers, discerning, compassionate, multi-taskers, and givers.
The list could go on and on. But when it comes to those things
passed down in our lives, such as generational curses or emotional
strongholds, which prove to be difficult for many in the family to
overcome, we don't like to talk about them.

My mom was open about our family's struggles and reinforced that we have a choice. Jesus' death made it possible for us to have a choice. However, we can't do it with our own strength. We have to follow the Holy Spirit through God's word and break every chain off of us through prayer and action. We can overcome alcoholism, depression, anxiety, sickness, negativity, gossip, slander, abuses of every kind, and selfishness, to name a few in my family lineage. Galatians 3 calls us into action to live by God's laws on our hearts, and therefore be made whole. He will deliver us from living under any of these curses that are not of Him so that we may be whole and be an example of what a relationship with Jesus looks like for others.

PRAYER

Heavenly Father, as I am loyal to You, You are so gracious to remove the things that would entrap me and pull me away from living for You and Your kingdom. Thank You for breaking every chain in my life. Show me now if there is anything that I need to bring into Your light to have You heal. I give You all the honor and praise for my freedom. In Jesus' name, amen.

BRAVE

Be strong and courageous, for you shall cause this people to inherit
the land that I swore to their fathers to give them.

JOSHUA 1:6 ESV

We can be brave and courageous in stepping out to do the things the Lord is asking us to do. Not because we are focused on our own strength, or lack thereof, but because the Lord tells us in Joshua that He is with us, just as He was with Moses. Every place that the soles of our feet touch, the Lord has given to us. As daughters of God, everywhere we go is God's territory. We must step out of our comfort zones and be brave, knowing that our Heavenly Father never leaves us, nor forsakes us, and gives us all that we need.

He supernaturally adds to everything that we are doing for His glory. The scripture above says that when we step out in faith, it isn't just for us but for all of God's people to inherit the things He has for them. We have to make our vision bigger to align with God's vision. This might mean leading well at work, being a faithful friend, not returning gossip for gossip, not doing drugs or getting drunk when everyone around us is, being sexually pure, showing unconditional love to people that don't deserve it (because we don't either), and following the path God has given us, even when we think it is beyond our ability.

PRAYER

Father, the stories You are weaving together for Your glory are beautiful and beyond what I could imagine or dream of. Help me to take my vision to Your place of supernatural provision, not just for me, but for everyone around me. Give me Your eyes and heart for Your people. I am grateful to be a part of the stories You are still writing for Your family. You alone make me brave. In Jesus' name, amen.

GREATEST
LOVE STORY

I am the vine; you are the branches. Whoever abides
in me and I in him, he it is that bears much fruit,
for apart from me you can do nothing.

JOSHUA 1:6 ESV

God's love is what makes it possible for us to bear fruit. Apart from Him, we cannot. When we ask Jesus into our hearts and we abide in Jesus, we will experience the greatest love story ever told and bear much fruit. The Bible tells us that we will have troubles and losses in this life. Sometimes, it can be overwhelming. However, when we abide and follow the directions our Father speaks to us, He takes us to new places of understanding and intimacy.

God ministers to my friend Christine through His presence and the hearts. Christine was in the process of buying her son's first car and discovered that the car was from this family's son,

who had just passed away due to heart issues. It was difficult for this family to let go of the car, and it was a process of grace for all involved. God laid it on Christine's heart to give the son's mother my first book, *A Royal Love Revealed: My Journey from Sorrow to God's Heart*, and to share with her the hope of the heart story. As Christine shared and gave her the book, the mother started to cry and clench something in her hand around her neck. Her husband had just given her the heart necklace, shown in the above photo, at Christmas. It read, "a piece of my heart is in heaven."

As she showed Christine her necklace, they were all in awe of God's love story for this husband and wife who lost their son so early. God had already sent His daughter a heart, and now He was sending His love story for her and her husband. God's presence and love shined bright in that moment for everyone, and it all started with Christine abiding in Jesus and doing what he asked her to do. This is the fruit from abiding with our Lord.

PRAYER

Heavenly Father, I will abide in You so that I may see the fruit of Your love in my life. You revive me with Your love. Your story is the greatest love story ever told. You work all things together for the good for those that love You. In Jesus' name, amen.

OUR ROCK
AND SALVATION

Everyone then who hears these words of mine and does them will
be like a wise man who built his house on the rock. And the rain
fell, and the floods came, and the winds blew and beat on that
house, but it did not fall, because it had been founded on the rock.

MATTHEW 7:24-25 ESV

I am sure all of us have felt these types of storms at some point
in our lives. It is a blessing to see the power of God in the lives of
those that have a strong foundation in the rock of Jesus, and who
are not swept away. Our rock is God Himself, and it is who He
is. He is our fortress, shield, stronghold, rock, refuge, the horn of
our salvation, and our deliverer. We have endurance and stability
when we are grounded in our Savior, who is the same today,
yesterday, and forever.

When our hearts are overwhelmed and unsure, we may find strength and rest from our rock, Jesus. He provides for us, spiritually, everything we need to stand firm and not be moved by the storms in this life. He is the only one that is immovable and perfect. I think, in these overwhelming moments, our tendency is self-reliance. But when we invite the Lord in to lead, plans beyond our imagination are possible. We may trust that as we seek and live by the rock of our salvation that we will see the splendor of His majesty. The things that we thought would hurt us are used to refine us and give us more vision for the path that leads to life.

PRAYER

Father, I humble myself to not only hear Your word, but to live by it. Holy Spirit, give me a clear understanding of Your word and let it fall on fertile soil in my heart as You build me up and place me on Your rock. I will rejoice in my storms because I know the strength of my rock. In Jesus' name, amen.

DWELLING WITH THE KING OF THE UNIVERSE

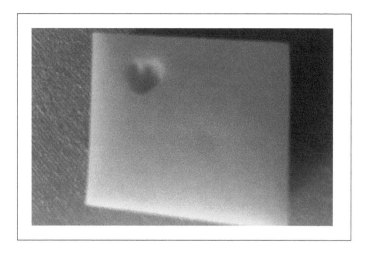

For you are a people holy to the Lord your God, and the
Lord has chosen you to be a people for his treasured possession,
out of all the peoples who are on the face of the earth.

DEUTERONOMY 14:2 ESV

We are a set-apart, sacred, and righteous people. Our God is
holy, and He says that we are holy to Him. Thankfully, the Lord
teaches us how to become holy people. The most important thing
that we need to choose each day is to dwell with our Heavenly
Father. By listening and posturing our hearts, we learn to receive
all that He has to say to us. This requires our time, just like our
relationships on earth.

The Lord guides us in Philippians 4 to strive for peace with everyone. *Strive* means "to fight for" and "to make great efforts to achieve." By praying and having a heart of thanksgiving, we may guard our hearts and minds in Christ Jesus. And, if anything is praiseworthy, focus on these thoughts; focus on whatever is true, honorable, just, pure, lovely, commendable, and excellent. Jesus doesn't leave us to guess or to just figure it out. These principles help us to stay focused and be a set-apart, holy people. Our Lord is the source, and now we have a choice to make about what we will focus on.

PRAYER

Heavenly Father, You are the holiness in me. My most treasured relationship is with You. Father, You are everything that is good in me. I want to dwell in the house of my Lord every day. Help me to focus on every praiseworthy thought and to shine Your love on those around me, making peace in my circle of influence. In Jesus' name, amen.

HEART
ON FIRE

I will sprinkle clean water on you, and you shall be clean from all
your uncleannesses, and from all your idols I will cleanse you. And
I will give you a new heart, and a new spirit I will put within you.
And I will remove the heart of stone from your flesh and give you a
heart of flesh. And I will put my Spirit within you, and cause you to
walk in my statutes and be careful to obey my rules.

EZEKIEL 36:25-27 ESV

The heart is the seat of our emotions. We should not be led by
our emotions, because they aren't always true. God's word says
that our hearts can deceive us and that every emotion, good and
bad, springs forth from it. However, when we receive the Lord,
He gives us a clean, new heart. We are able to be led by His word
because our hearts know Him and trust His word for putting our

emotions in check. The Lord is so faithful and gives us a heart and mind to grow in our faith.

We are saved in our faith when we believe Jesus within our minds and trust within our hearts. When Jesus walked the earth, His mission was to fulfill the law and restore the heart of man through a relationship with God, not just by keeping laws. We are fully awake and able, body and spirit, when our hearts are burning with Jesus' love and truth. It is like a fire that is not easily extinguished.

PRAYER

Heavenly Father, the value You place on me, through Your love and truth when You speak to me, is like a fire that cannot be put out. The disciples explained that when they broke bread with You and when You opened up the scriptures to them, their hearts burned. Open my eyes to You. Let my heart burn for You and Your desires. In Jesus' name, amen.

OUR
COMPASS

Send out your light and your truth; let them lead me; let them
bring me to your holy hill and to your dwelling!

PSALM 43:3 ESV

In the message version of this scripture, the word *lantern* is used
for *light* and *compass* is used for *truth*. The word of God is our
compass. We have an instructional book of life that will guide
our paths. We might feel like we are going in the right direction,
but we must ask, is it God's direction? When we are in a season
of increase and everything seems to be working out for us,
sometimes, we may forget the Lord. We fall away from following
the Lord's statutes and commands, and before we know it, we do
not remember that the increase came from our Lord. He alone
should be given the glory, not our proud hearts.

When we eat and are full and have all that we need, God still calls us to His purposes for us to reach His people for the eternal kingdom. Let's not stop there. In these moments, Deuteronomy 8 warns us to not say in our hearts that we have gained wealth by our power and might. This scripture says that it is God who gives us the power to attain wealth so that He may confirm His promises with His family. God's truth will order our footsteps, and He will give us the ability to fulfill the call on our lives, for our own achievements and for the Lord's glory.

PRAYER

Father, You are the light of the world. There are many things that try to pull me in different directions and away from You. Fasten my thoughts on every miraculous, truthful word You give me. Your lantern and compass enable me to follow wherever You lead. I give You all the praise and honor. Thank You for Your peace. In Jesus' name, amen.

DAUGHTERS WITH CHARACTER

Her children rise up and call her blessed; her husband also, and he praises her: "Many women have done excellently, but you surpass them all." Charm is deceitful, and beauty is vain, but a woman who fears the Lord is to be praised. Give her of the fruit of her hands, and let her works praise her in the gates.

PROVERBS 31:28-31 ESV

Daughters with character know the power of unity. A spirit that is quiet and submitted to God has power over the enemy like nothing else. God's grace rests upon His daughters in exchange for their humility. Our fears are outweighed by our respect and honor for God. When God's daughters are awakened to fulfill God's purposes, our character is shaped and our hearts learn that we have an assignment.

All of the areas in our hearts and minds that need to be renewed happen through a reverential fear of the Lord. Once daughters experience trust and loyalty with Jesus, and the fruit of it, they cannot deny the overflow of benefits in all of their relationships. Young women that give honor to everyone around them receive more than they give. A daughter of character is strong, only rising up to lift up those around her. She seeks peace with everyone and uses her words to build up others. Scripture teaches us that what we sow, we will reap. We can all be daughters of character because of our Heavenly Father.

PRAYER

Father, I want to live as a daughter of character. Show me how to use my words for building up those around me. Show me how to be gracious, humble, and generous. You are the source of all that is good and pure. You call me lovely and give me Your peace. Guide me in Your grace to understand that when I bridle my tongue, I am sowing everlasting fruit. In these moments, heaven and earth kiss. Righteousness and peace have come together. In Jesus' name, amen.

CREATE HARMONY
THROUGH WISDOM

Go to the ant, O sluggard; consider her ways, and be wise.
Without having any chief, officer, or ruler, she prepares her
bread in summer and gathers her food in harvest.

PROVERBS 6:6-8 ESV

My friend Michelle walked out to her back porch to see a heart-shaped ant pile. The Lord quickly brought to my mind the message of the ants in the Bible and how God points us to their ways. The ants teach us about having a plan and doing our part. This creates order and harmony. There is no time to complain, because they are busy doing what they're supposed to do, so they don't have time to fight amongst themselves. Everyone is responsible and they get a lot done in peace.

Ants have incredible strength. They can carry between ten and fifty times their own body weight and run approximately 300 meters per hour. God instructs us to learn from His creation in the book of Job. How much more can we, as God's people, push through limitations and hardships? God holds all wisdom and strength, and He has counsel and understanding. The things God asks us to do, no matter how hard, may be attained because of His Holy Spirit, who brings us unimaginable layers of blessings as we trust Him in the process.

PRAYER

Heavenly Father, give me Your strength and wisdom. I can be strong and give what is in my hand because of the Holy Spirit who lives in me. I praise You for every blessing in my life. I look back and am blown away by Your faithfulness in my life. I look to today for an opportunity to fulfill what You are asking me to do for Your glory. Thank You for the gift of Your great wisdom! In Jesus' name, amen.

PROMISES
OF GOD

And I will make them and the places all around my
hill a blessing, and I will send down the showers in their
season; they shall be showers of blessing."
EZEKIEL 34:26 ESV

We can hold fast to the promises of God and our hope because
of His sovereignty. God's promises do not change. Our hope
is not in other people making things better, or our changing
circumstances. God's showers of blessings over our homes happen
in His sovereign timing. We do not deny reality, but cling to the
promises of God until the timing is right. I shared the heart story
with someone I had just met, and to my surprise, the Lord had
shown her hearts since she was a teenager.

How gracious and faithful that the Lord spoke to His daughter at such a young age in this way. He whispered His love and security to her through the hearts. While she was reading my first book, she went for a walk on the beach and found all of those heart shells. God blessed us both by bringing us into each other's lives in His timing. We may be encouraged and confirmed by God's promises in limitless ways. The hearts are just one way He is revealing love and mercy. When we look for Christ, we will find Him.

PRAYER

Heavenly Father, thank You that Your promises for me never fade. To look and find You is a treasure of confidence and security that no matter what I face, You will provide. Divine favor is given to me in every area of my life. I will walk like I am set free, because I am. In Jesus' name, amen.

I'M FOREVER
THE LORD'S

I will sing of the steadfast love of the Lord,
forever; with my mouth I will make known your
faithfulness to all generations.

PSALM 89:1 ESV

God made us for love and for us to be loved by Him. Scripture says that the Lord's steadfast love will be built up forever and that in the heavens He establishes His faithfulness. His covenant with us is love. Through the Lord's love, He takes all of our broken pieces and puts together a story of complete love and faithfulness. He promises to never remove His love from us, even when we violate His commandments.

We should want even more to be faithful to the Lord and walk as children of the light. There are always consequences for our choices. That is why we should choose wisely. Jesus rules with love and justice. When we see and meet the goodness of God, it should compel us, in return, to be forever His. We may be set free and receive an eternal embrace from our Heavenly Father, who makes us keenly aware of paradise and its means. This heart photo was a gift while driving down the road at just the right time.

PRAYER

Heavenly Father, You are Lord of all and work all things together for my good. When I encounter Your faithfulness, it is so profound. You know the best way to love me and draw me closer to You. I am honored to share who You are and Your faithfulness. I will rejoice in the song of Your love for me forever. In Jesus' name, amen.

BEAR GOD'S IMAGE
THROUGH FAITH

For we are his workmanship, created in
Christ Jesus for good works, which God prepared
beforehand, that we should walk in them.

EPHESIANS 2:10 ESV

One morning I was talking with my daughter about fear, about
stepping out in total trust in God, and that the gifts He gives us
are for bearing witness to His image. As we were getting up from
our breakfast table, I saw a dead leaf in a plant. When I went to
pluck it out, this heart was on top of it. My heart skipped a beat,
and we both sat in awe of our God. He reassured my daughter, in
that moment, that His words are true.

Each of us was created for such a time as this, for good works to bear the image of Christ. When we feel unqualified, we need to remember that the Lord's word is where we find all that we need to bear His image. He builds us up, piece by piece, rewriting our story for His glory. Jesus is the only King that has ever left his throne to lay His life down for each of us. And He is the only King that defeated death and gave eternal life. I pray that we encounter God today and that we open our hearts to receive His relentless love. No matter where we are or how we feel, we have a purpose today for the good works God created for each of us to do.

PRAYER

Heavenly Father, I want to bear Your image each day. I want to point others toward Your faithfulness and the plans that You have prepared for them. I can only walk by faith when my mind and heart are set on You. Today, fill me with faith through Your grace. I can have faith over fear when in Your love. In Jesus' name, amen.

DIVINE
DESIGN

For his invisible attributes, namely, his eternal
power and divine nature, have been clearly perceived,
ever since the creation of the world, in the things that
have been made. So they are without excuse.

ROMANS 1:20 ESV

The photo above is of beach sand from the Florida Keys that
has been magnified. Creation reveals God's glory and majesty.
We get to see how specific and exact the inner workings of
creation are, as it is divine design! Our souls can only be restored
by the divine nature of God. Romans warns that those who put
their faith in mortal man, instead of an immortal God, have
no excuse, because He has made it clear. When we choose to

turn away from the testimony of the Lord, our hearts become darkened and chase impurity.

We can try to claim wisdom, but the only true wisdom is God's, which changes our souls by shifting our worship from our flesh to the Creator. We gain the Lord's perfect law, which extends to wisdom, a joyous heart, enlightened eyes, pureness, and truth. The mystery of godliness is great indeed. And in keeping it, there is great reward. God calls us His daughters, and for us to be a light for the world to shine His character.

PRAYER

Father, You are my redeemer. I am vindicated and pleasing to You when I walk in Your commandments. As Your daughter, I am a pillar of Your truth. Restore my soul, day by day, and lead me in Your living testimonies so that I may keep a clean heart that meditates on You. In Jesus' name, amen.

BE
FAITHFUL

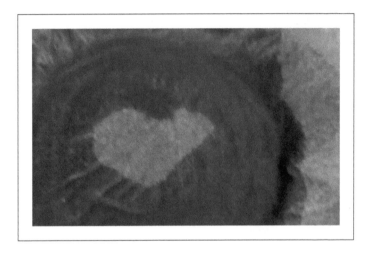

If we have died with him, we will also live with him; if we endure, we
will also reign with him; if we deny him, he also will deny us; if we
are faithless, he remains faithful—for he cannot deny himself.

2 TIMOTHY 2:11-13 ESV

God extends His faithfulness to every son and daughter in the
midst of daily tasks. No matter what hardship you face today,
know that the faithful one, Jesus, is still moving on your behalf.
The wonders of Jesus and His faithfulness are breathtaking.
Sometimes, we get to see it, and sometimes, it stays in the unseen.
He is never unfaithful and is always with us, waiting for us to, in

DAY 61

return, be faithful to Him. When we are faithful to God, He is faithful to us. What can we do today to be faithful to Him?

We don't need to blend in or follow someone else's calling. God has given each one of us a flame for Him and His purposes that only He can fan. Through prayer, we can give the special gift of love God has given to us, in order to bring faith, hope, and love to our circle of influence. Second Timothy says that God does not give us a spirit of fear, but of love, power, and self-control. No matter what we suffer, if we suffer for God's purposes, then we gain faith and love in Christ.

PRAYER

Heavenly Father, miracle maker, thank You for always being faithful to me. Help me, today, to be faithful to You in everything I do. I entrust my future to Jesus, the author and finisher of my faith. I do not operate out of fear, but out of love, power, and a sound mind. I have the mind of Christ, and every thought I take captive to the truth of God's word. In Jesus' name, amen.

MAY WE NEVER LOSE
OUR WONDER

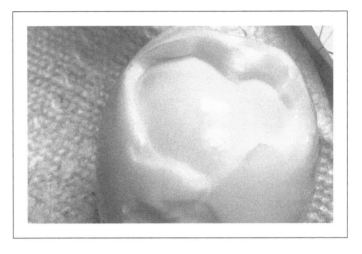

Although he was a son, he learned obedience through
what he suffered. And being made perfect, he became the
source of eternal salvation to all who obey him.

HEBREWS 5:8-9 ESV

May we never lose our wonder and always be like a child, staring at our King's beautiful ways. Open the eyes of our hearts to see You, God. Everything that God is doing through the hearts is heavenly. I am thankful that my mom lost her religion decades ago and decided to find out who Jesus really is. No masks and no performance. She found something different, and that difference was a relationship with Jesus.

When she went to eternity, I learned how to receive God's love in deeper ways. We all experience suffering because we live in a fallen world, full of sin. We can learn obedience through the things we suffer with Christ. Through our obedience, God has His perfect work in us, healing us. We are able to not be victims, throw blame, or carry unforgiveness and bitterness. Our focus can shift from the pain itself to the one who takes away our pain, Jesus, who is the rescue and miracle. And He waits at every turn in our days to show us His wonder and salvation.

PRAYER

Heavenly Father, may I never lose my wonder in You, King Jesus. Your love consumes me and compels me to give my life back to You in obedience. You are my rescue, and I gladly suffer for Your name's sake. Strengthen me and my community of faith and deliver us from evil. In Jesus' name, amen.

GOD'S GLORY

He loves righteousness and justice; the earth is full of the
steadfast love of the Lord. By the word of the Lord the heavens
were made, and by the breath of his mouth all their host.

PSALM 33:5-6 ESV

This heart in the Grand Canyon is a reminder of God's creation
and how He speaks to us through it. God spoke all of creation
into existence. He spoke, and it was done. How incredible it is
that the Lord's counsel stands forever. The ages were framed
by the word of God. Blessed are the ones that receive God's
inheritance and deliverance. I can look back on my life and see
how God has shaped my heart.

God is in every detail of sculpting each of our hearts. Take a moment to think back over the times in your life where He kept and guided you, and give Him thanks. How can we turn to the Lord today and experience His love that He has for each of us? When we take this pause, we are able to see His tapestry of love that He is weaving into our hearts, out of God's glory. There is no one and nothing that can stop the plans of the Lord for the ages.

PRAYER

Father, I give You all the glory for the love that You have poured into my heart. I cannot boast in my own abilities, because I know every healed part of my heart is from my Father in heaven. Lord, hear the cries of my heart and bring wholeness to the areas of my heart that need healing. When I cannot see, open my eyes to Your unfailing love. In Jesus' name, amen.

LAY YOUR BURDENS ON THE LORD

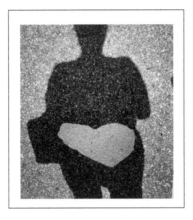

"My grace is sufficient for you, for my power is made perfect in weakness." Therefore I will boast all the more gladly of my weaknesses, so that the power of Christ may rest upon me.

2 CORINTHIANS 12:9 ESV

My friend Tammy has sent me too many heart photos to count. The Lord has ministered to her and her grandson through the hearts. The heart story has even touched the hearts of some of her family members. God confirms His tender loving care. Seeing God's grace on the move is the most powerful thing I have ever witnessed. Tammy has stood in the gap, praying for those in her family, and has relied on her God through many difficult circumstances. She and her husband are raising their

grandson, and also praying and believing for her daughter to be set free from addiction.

We all have burdens and things that we wish we could change for those that we love. God loves them more than we can imagine, and He can carry our burdens. The Lord tells us to lay our burdens down on Him. He will be everything that we need. We can rise up and be strong when we are weak because His power rests on us. Our Heavenly Father is so kind to love us, so personally, as we put our trust in Him. He is moving in the silence and never leaves us. I pray that He gives you rest today, and even when your questions aren't answered swiftly that His love and power rest on you through it all.

PRAYER

Father, I praise You because Your grace is sufficient for me. Your love reaches to every corner of my aching heart. I trust You with all of my worries and burdens. I want to stand in Your love, no matter what I face today, and experience Your supernatural grace. I will boast in my weaknesses because it is then that I experience Your power. In Jesus' name, amen.

A CHILD
OF GOD

Whoever has my commandments and keeps them, he it is
who loves me. And he who loves me will be loved by my Father,
and I will love him and manifest myself to him.

JOHN 14:21 ESV

My husband, Erik, took one bite out of the apple in the photo
above. Erik's father had gained heaven during that week.
Throughout the week, the Lord showed His love and made
Himself plain for Erik to know and see. Our Heavenly Father
and the priests of heaven ministered to us as we honored Erik's
dad, Vaughn. When we become children of God, we know that

He is for us. In everything we face, we know that He is going before us and, at the same time, is with us.

The Lord is for us and wants to deposit His peace into our hearts today. All of heaven is moving on our behalf daily. When we have nowhere to give the love that we once had for someone who leaves this earth, we may give it to God. When we pour out all of our grief and pain at the feet of Jesus, He refills us with His fierce, consuming love that holds us in an indescribable embrace. It is one of the mysteries of His grace. Hallelujah! Let us give Him all the praise and glory forever.

PRAYER

Heavenly Father, I am Your child. You have a seat at Your table just for me. I gladly keep Your commandments that You have written on my heart. I choose Your embrace of love and intimacy that You have for me every hour of every day. Thank You for making Yourself plain to see. Remove the blinders from my eyes to receive and know Your love. In Jesus' name, amen.

BEAR WITH
ONE ANOTHER

Bear one another's burdens, and so fulfill the law of Christ.

GALATIANS 6:2 ESV

Do you believe the goodness of God is running after you? Have you laid your life down for Him? We have to surrender in order to be led. I look back and think how faithful God has been. His kind voice has led me to places of calmness and truth in the darkest times. He is the Shepherd of our hearts and wants to guide us to places of safety and fullness. We lack nothing in our Shepherd's presence. Our souls are being carried in our Father's arms, arms that do not fail. For those that sow in the Spirit will reap eternal life.

Let us not grow weary from doing good. The Lord calls us to walk with the people in our lives like we walk with our Shepherd. To petition to our Lord in prayer, on their behalf, is an honor. To speak our Father's living words into our friends' and family's lives agrees with all of heaven and the heart of our Lord. He wants to lead us, by His Spirit, in goodness. Beautiful things happen when we put others before our own needs. The heart photo above was one of many seen as women were coming together to pray for a friend who was experiencing loss. Thank You, Jesus, for always reaching for us and daring us to believe how much we are loved by You.

PRAYER

Heavenly Father, I can sow into the Spirit because of Your presence in my life. I am loved by You, and You have only safe places to guide me. Your kind words bear witness to who You are as my Father. I trust that You are working all things together for Your plans to prosper all of Your children. Help me to see today how I can put others before myself and share the love that You have so generously poured out for me. In Jesus' name, amen.

HIS BANNER OVER
US IS LOVE

Let it be known to you therefore, brothers, that through
this man forgiveness of sins is proclaimed to you, and by him
everyone who believes is freed from everything from which
you could not be freed by the law of Moses.

ACTS 13:38-39 ESV

Everyone who receives Christ is freed from every sin and emotional
stronghold. Receiving requires action on our part, the act of
belief. We have to put our faith into action and do the things that
God is calling us to do, or it wouldn't be faith. Galatians 5 adds
that for our freedom, Christ has set us free, so we need to stand
firm and not submit again to a yoke of slavery. Scripture shows
us that we have a choice in what we submit to. When we submit
to things that are godless, out of fear or what feels comfortable,
God's word provides a way out through a relationship with Him.

DAY 67

We are supernaturally given Jesus' strength to choose His ways and be free.

We have choices before us every day, to choose the King's offerings or the enemy's. If it doesn't line up with God's living word that brings life, peace, and joy, no matter the circumstances, then it's holding us back from wholeness. We can either have wings of freedom or be grounded with weights of emotional strongholds. Jesus made it possible for us to rise up and sit at the Lord's table, to be in the house of the Lord while we are here on earth. Real love is a choice. We must choose wisely and see what God does in our lives. We are sustained and refreshed in our Heavenly Father's embrace for all of our days. Song of Solomon 2:4 describes, so beautifully, "He brought me to the banqueting house, and his banner over me was love."

PRAYER

Father, I do not want to be fooled into following the distractions the enemy throws my way. I want to dwell in the house of my Father and receive all of Your benefits on earth. I know that what I do here on earth is tied to what I will do in eternity. Draw me, with Your lovingkindness and truth, toward the path of freedom You have laid out before me. In Jesus' name, amen.

ETERNAL
LOVE

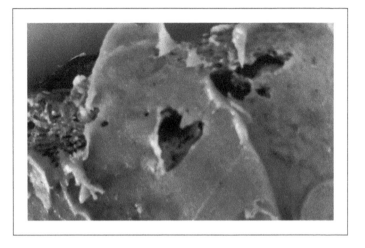

Have I not commanded you? Be strong and courageous.
Do not be frightened, and do not be dismayed, for the
Lord your God is with you wherever you go.

JOSHUA 1:9 ESV

I have countless photos of moments spent with King Jesus from my daughter, Loren, and her friends. I can't help but thank God for His ever-present love. He speaks and shows His love to us through the hearts. He told me nine years ago to look for the hearts when I prayed for Him to draw nearer to me after my mom went to eternity. Since then, God's message of love and presence has reached so many through the hearts. The hearts have become such a powerful testimony of Jesus' presence and love for His people. Each moment has a purpose from King

Jesus. His heart is speaking to the heart of His most valued creation, His sons and daughters.

We try so hard to understand God's ways, but it is impossible. Our minds are too limited to grasp the limitlessness of our King. If we just pause in these moments and receive whatever it is God is speaking to us, we will be forever encouraged by a loving God. It is incredible that our God's love dips down into our humanity and says, *I love you* and *I see you.* He sees us in our struggles and says, *I love you* and *I see where I want to take you. Follow Me to places of peace and refreshment.* It is powerful to grasp that we are never alone and that all of heaven is fighting for our hearts to return and be kept by Jesus.

PRAYER

Heavenly Father, thank You for extending Your grace through the hearts. You have endless paths to reach my heart. I cannot begin to understand the vastness of Your influence on my life. But I can praise You and receive every God-given moment of love and power that brings me to a place of wholeness. In Jesus' name, amen.

ONE GOD AND FATHER OF ALL

One God and Father of all,
who is over all and through all and in all.
EPHESIANS 4:6 ESV

He is a Father of all and is working all things together for our good. But we must do our part to receive and trust Jesus. God is the only one who can bring beauty from the ashes in our lives. We can get better, instead of bitter, through the things we suffer. In the day-to-day battles, we may choose to be like clay in the potter's hand, which are the hands of Jesus. If we will repent and turn away from evil, God will build us up from the ashes and turn our stubborn hearts into humble hearts, enabling us to follow His voice. Our Father's voice is for everyone to hear, and He draws everyone to it for a relationship with Him.

The Holy Spirit helps us to be changed, from glory to glory. Second Corinthians 3 instructs us that where the Spirit of the Lord is, there is freedom. Our freedom enables us to see clearly the glory of the Lord and be transformed into His image, as the Holy Spirit sees us. I can't help but to think of all the storms this rock has weathered in Maui. And in the center of it, a heart was formed.

Jesus wants to do the miraculous in our lives every day. When we open our hearts to Him, that is exactly what He will do through every circumstance we may face. It is beyond our comprehension that we have a Father who loves each of us so much that He is in every detail of our lives. Our Heavenly Father is limitless and perfect in every way, and He generously pours out His inheritance for His children.

PRAYER

Heavenly Father, I praise You for every good thing that rests in my heart. I may be encouraged knowing that You are over all, through all, and in all. This truth leaves nothing out. Help me, today, to surrender my heart to You, Lord, so that You may mold me into the person You made me to be. I praise You and give You all the honor for bringing beauty from the ashes in my life. In Jesus' name, amen.

TURNING
TOWARD GOD

I will give them a heart to know that I am the Lord,
and they shall be my people and I will be their God,
for they shall return to me with their whole heart.

JEREMIAH 24:7 ESV

I would like to share with you a sacred story from my friend
Hannah. We met at our church, where I shared with her the
heart story, my journey from sorrow to God's heart. A few weeks
later, she saw her first heart right before receiving some difficult
news about her pregnancy with her second child, Malachi. Their
family and friends stood with Hannah and her husband in prayer
for their son to be born healthy and whole. Sometimes, things
don't work out the way we expect—but for God. Fast forward
many months later, Malachi was born, prematurely and with
some health complications. After fifteen precious hours with his
parents, he went to be with Jesus. Hannah shared how beautiful
Malachi was and that he looked like an angel.

As hard as that day was for them, God showed her several
hearts, within hours of each other. Her favorite was when she

was leaving the beach, and she saw three heart-shaped leaves. In between them, there was a leaf that looked like angel wings. Hannah was incredibly comforted by these and thought of them as God's whispers of hope and promise. A few days later, the Lord met her with additional hearts. Hannah shared that she wanted to cry, but that God's overflowing love brought her such peace and joy in these moments.

Revelations teaches us that we will overcome all of the brokenness we experience by the blood of our Lamb, who was slain, and the word of our testimony. Hannah is sharing her testimony to help others know the love of God, no matter what pain they may face. He wants to be in that pain and carry it for them. God wants to reach His people through us, to bring love and wholeness by sharing our testimonies. I am happy to share that Hannah found out she was pregnant while I was writing this book. There is no greater love than the love of the Father, and no matter what our answers look like, His promises are true.

PRAYER

Heavenly Father, thank You for dying on the cross so that I may be free. I am grateful for Your loving kindness that draws me to You and all of Your promises. One day, every tear will be wiped away from my eyes, and all that I have lost will be restored. Until then, thank You for carrying me and holding me together in Your love. In Jesus' name, amen.

SAFE HAVEN

Then they were glad that the waters were quiet, and he brought them to their desired haven. Let them thank the Lord for his steadfast love, for his wondrous works to the children of man!

PSALM 107:30-31 ESV

The above photo is a sea anemone in the shape of a heart, photographed at an aquarium in Atlantic Beach, Florida. The sea anemone is a safe haven for some of the fish in the ocean. The fish are protected from predators and they have a safe place to rest. We can expect the same thing when we live for King Jesus. Our loyalty and trust in God springs forth rivers in a desert and warmth in winter. Have you ever been in situations where you feel dry and thirsty in a rainstorm, or it feels like winter in the middle of summer?

There are people and situations that don't extend love, but rather harshness. These experiences are beyond our control because we can only be responsible for ourselves. If we are honest, the only good in us is from the one who is love, God. Those that inhabit evil, the Lord will let live in a parched and dry land, without a safe haven. But how miraculous is our God that, no matter where we tread, we can have a safe haven of refreshment and fruitfulness, wherever we may stand. It is by the Lord's blessing that we can multiply in every area of our lives and produce lasting fruit that does not wither but is a safe haven, kept by the steadfast love of our God.

PRAYER

Dear Heavenly Father, I want to be a person that extends Your living waters to those around me. You are the goodness in me, and I praise You for Your faithfulness in giving me a safe haven, no matter where I go. I ask for Your refreshment when I'm in need of refuge from the harshness in this world. In Jesus' name, amen.

THE MAJESTY
OF THE LORD

The earth was without form and void, and darkness
was over the face of the deep. And the Spirit of God
was hovering over the face of the waters.

GENESIS 1:2 ESV

God is the Alpha and Omega! The beginning and the end. The earth was void and without form, before God spoke it into being. He created man in His image so that He would have a family. Isaiah 40 describes the majesty of the Lord. The Lord measured the waters and heaven with His hand, calculated the dust of the earth, weighed the mountains in scales, and the hills in balances. The nations are like small bits of dust to Him. It is God who sits above the earth, since the foundations of it. His majesty cannot be compared.

And, yet, He calls creation and its inhabitants out by name. By the Lord's might and power, no one is missing from Him. It is beyond our comprehension to understand that our God never grows weary, and His understanding is unsearchable. He is the one who gives each of His daughter's power and strength. It is hard to wait on the Lord. Many of us struggle with waiting. But, in this waiting, when we learn about the majesty of our King and we experience His gifts, we will gladly wait on the Lord. He will renew our strength, and we will run our good race and not grow weary. Our youth will be renewed, like the eagles. I saw this heart hovering over the ocean as I was praying to God to guide me in the waiting.

PRAYER

Heavenly Father, it is comforting to know how close You are to Your people. Your greatness and care are beyond my comprehension. Today, I ask You to show me Your presence in my life. I want to know You more and be strengthened through Your power. Holy Spirit, invade my space today. Give me ears to hear and eyes to see Your love that surrounds me. In Jesus' name, amen.

NO SHAME

For am I now seeking the approval of man, or of God?
Or am I trying to please man? If I were still trying to
please man, I would not be a servant of Christ.
GALATIANS 1:10 ESV

Take a moment and ask God to show you if you are living to please anyone other than God. Or, to bring to your memory all the times in your life where you chose to please God, not others. God sees, He knows, and He calls us to His higher ground. No matter how many times we mess up, He is there to guide us back and help us get stronger. We are living in a world where people find it admirable to shame others. Jesus didn't come to shame us; He came to serve us and guide us with His love. We are each set apart for the good works God has prepared for us. My friend Shera has had to stand firm and trust God through some very difficult circumstances, and the Holy Spirit has guided her faithfully. These hearts appeared on the plane window as she was flying for a work trip.

DAY
73

We are here for God's delight and to help each other find our way back to Him. We have a best friend in the Holy Spirit, who speaks specifically to each of our hearts for what we need individually. The most important thing we can do is listen to Him. Which means that each of us will have a different peace, due to different things, as we walk by faith. It is not up to us to judge what others do. God will judge everyone, according to His truths.

Walking by faith doesn't always make sense in our limited minds, but if we know God has asked us to do something, then we need to do it. There are blessings and opened doors that have no end when we are obedient. There are also consequences for when we turn our backs on God and choose to please people, instead of our Creator. Romans 5:5 tells us, "Hope does not put us to shame, because God's love has been poured into our hearts through the Holy Spirit who has been given to us."

PRAYER

Heavenly Father, help me to encourage those around me in their walk with You. When doubt and questions flood my mind, remove them from me and guide me to prayer for building others up. I release false responsibility for the things that are only meant for You to care for. Remove shame from my heart and give me Your peace that surpasses all understanding. In Jesus' name, amen.

THE LORD'S FAVOR

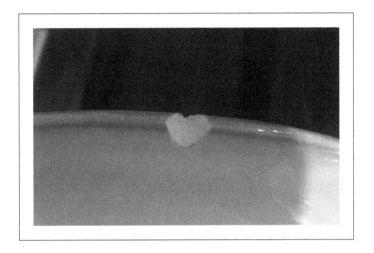

They shall build up the ancient ruins; they shall
raise up the former devastations; they shall repair the ruined cities,
the devastations of many generations.

ISAIAH 61:4 ESV

When we feel like things are ruined or devastated beyond repair,
God often says, I *am preparing hearts and minds through the
struggles.* For those that know the Lord, we can trust that He is
working for us, and we are able to stand in faith and wait on the
Lord's timing. The favor of the Lord makes it possible for us to
not lose hope and to be kept. When we keep walking with Jesus
and our eyes are on Him, He will bring us through to restoration.
My friend Christine was disappointed about chipping her bowl,
but she quickly saw it was in the shape of a heart.

The Lord's favor does not always come in the package that we want. More times than not, it is through some sort of circumstance that requires us to have faith and wait. Keep waiting, even when things don't change. Little by little, you are receiving all God has for you. It is amazing to see how God knows our hearts and knows the way to continue to grow them and mold them into His image. It is easy for us to trust in what we know and leave God out of our plans. But I think that many of us can attest to the fact that when we do stop ourselves and put God first, we are amazed by the hand of God and the miracles He does in our lives.

PRAYER

Heavenly Father, thank You for turning my devastation into blessings. In Your kingdom, there is nothing wasted or lost. I want the promises of Your kingdom come and Your will to be done in my life. Give me Your eyes to see more clearly, as I trust in the favor of my Lord. In Jesus' name, amen.

ENCOUNTERING THE
LOVE OF GOD

And you, who were dead in your trespasses and the
uncircumcision of your flesh, God made alive together
with him, having forgiven us all our trespasses, by canceling
the record of debt that stood against us with its legal demands.
This he set aside, nailing it to the cross.
COLOSSIANS 2:13-14 ESV

I enjoy receiving heart photos from friends and hearing about how God has encouraged them. We can live our lives hidden in Christ, strengthened by our faith, and overflowing with thankfulness. God nailed our inequities to the cross. There is no debt against our souls when we receive Jesus into our hearts through salvation. So often, we stop there, but God continues to call us to be full in Christ Jesus here on earth as well. We become fully alive in Christ. Religion, and its rules and judgements, does not stop the sin in our flesh.

The love of Christ is what turns our hearts to follow Christ and refuse the desires of our flesh. Have you ever encountered the love of God? How do we know if we have encountered God's love? We know because we are never the same. The Lord's word gives life because it is alive. A relationship with Jesus is an open door for anyone who will walk through it. Jesus enlarges our hearts with joy when we follow His commandments. Psalm 119 teaches us, "I will run the course of Your commandments, for you shall enlarge my heart." Isaiah 60 also says that when we know God, "then you shall see and be radiant; your heart shall thrill and exult." While on vacation, just before moving their family across the country in faith, our friends saw the heart on this horse.

PRAYER

Heavenly Father, Your laws are written on my heart. I find freedom when I do things Your way and receive Your love. Remove doubt and fear from me and replace them with Your joy. There is no more debt owed when I am saved through Christ. Help me to know Your truth and confidently walk the course You have made for me in my relationship with Jesus. In Jesus' name, amen.

PURSUE
HONOR

There are six things that the Lord hates, seven that
are an abomination to him: haughty eyes, a lying tongue, and
hands that shed innocent blood, a heart that devises wicked plans,
feet that make haste to run to evil, a false witness who breathes
out lies, and one who sows discord among brothers.

PROVERBS 6:16-19 ESV

Offense is an enemy of our hearts. Keeping offense in our hearts
is what grows these things that the Lord hates. As mentioned
above in scripture, these things are gossip, division, liars, pride
and superiority, murder, and enjoying cutting down other people.
If we are to be imagers of Christ, then we cannot have offense in
our hearts. Offense is a trap to deceive us out of the fullness of
God and unity in His perfect love.

What we pursue matters. When we understand all that we need is in Christ, we do not have the desire to attack and disrespect others to feel better about ourselves. Things that are worthy of our pursuit are righteousness, kindness, and honor in everything we do. These will produce overflow in every area of our lives. And God will redeem all that is lost in the physical. It is God's design for His people to learn how to love one another and experience His abundance in their lives daily. Even when cutting open a tomato, God is moving to confirm and honor those He loves.

PRAYER

Father, I want to pursue honor in everything I do. Jesus is the example for me on how to treat others that might feel like a threat to me or those that are suffering and looked down upon by society. Stop my feet and mouth from treading on mischievous ground. I want to be known for being a peacekeeper and encouraging those around me to live in Your ways. I pray against offense entering into my heart. In Jesus' name, amen.

SWEETNESS TO
THE SOUL

Gracious words are like a honeycomb,
sweetness to the soul and health to the body.
PROVERBS 16:24 ESV

We can choose to be a work of preservation or destruction in
our lives and in the lives of others. The Holy Spirit is always
at work. These hearts were on the door at a school where our
church, Celebration Orlando, has Sunday services. Faith comes
by hearing the word of God. And when we hear the word of
God, it is activated in our lives by listening and applying it to our
lives. God calls us to not only be planted in the church, but to be
the church wherever we go. When darkness surrounds us, Jesus is
still the light of the world and with us. The Lord's graciousness
in us should impart value and honor.

When we think of the story of Judas in the Bible, we may ask ourselves, why in the world would he betray Jesus? He saw who Jesus was, including His miracles, and he had a relationship with Him. But, just like us, sometimes, things don't go our way, or we don't like how things are unfolding in our lives. We don't see God's graciousness yet, and we may become angry at God, out of disappointment. The fact is that following Jesus isn't always easy, and we cannot always understand His ways of doing things. This is when we are the most vulnerable, when we can choose to either turn toward Jesus or away from Him. We may not always understand God's plans, but we can always *trust* His plans.

PRAYER

Heavenly Father, Your word tells me to trust You, and when I do, my heart rejoices in Your salvation and unfailing love. I want to turn to You in times of trial and disappointment and speak words that are healthy to the body of Christ. Help me to grow in my endurance in the things that I cannot change. I know that You are for me and came to give me a future and hope. In Jesus' name, amen.

GRACE AND MERCY

And the men marveled, saying, "What sort of man is this,
that even winds and sea obey him?"
MATTHEW 8:27 ESV

God's word says that He gives rain on the earth and sends forth
the water on the fields. The Lord speaks to the wind, and it rises
and descends. Noah, in his time, was thought of as an extremist.
Walking by faith requires us to act in obedience when it makes no
sense because we can't see it yet. We walk by faith, not by sight.
The hearts of men were wicked in Noah's time, and the Lord had
to stop all of the evil on the earth. He is a God of judgement and
salvation. We have the same choice before us today in a world
full of evil and hate. God uses all of creation to draw people to
Himself. The hearts are just one example of His grace and mercy.

We can choose to trust Jesus and walk by faith and redemption, no matter what other people think, or we can choose judgement before God. Our unity with Christ is what makes us righteous and gives us the ability to keep our hearts from wickedness. How beautiful is this rainbow with two palm trees below it forming a heart? God's promises are true and available to each one of us in every storm and flood that life brings us. When we believe in the power and provision of God, His living waters will continuously flow from our hearts. God created the rainbow to remind all of His creation of His covenant, which means that He will never again flood the earth. The world needs the hope, truth, and love of Christ. We need to continue the work of His covenant and help each other return to their first love.

PRAYER

Heavenly Father, Your grace and mercy chase me down. I want to receive Your salvation today, no matter what I face. I want to walk by faith and not by sight. If all of creation obeys Your voice, then so will I. Thank You for calming the storms in my life. Show me the way of escape, and I will gladly take it, even when it doesn't make sense. In Jesus' name, amen.

THE GOODNESS
OF GOD

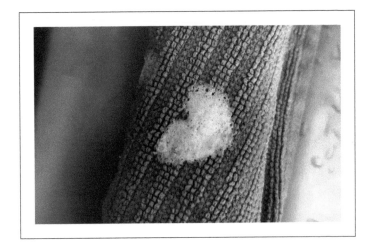

Commit your work to the Lord, and your plans will be established.

PROVERBS 16:3 ESV

I am so glad that I do not have to worry or stress about other people's hearts. God knows each one of our hearts, so there is no outwitting or fooling the Lord. Frequently, when we become Christ followers, we feel that it is our job to judge others. It is not our job, but the Lord's alone. God calls us to be vessels of righteousness. We are to speak truth, in love, guiding people to our Heavenly Father. The Holy Spirit is the only one who can change hearts. We do not carry that responsibility and should not be led by our emotions, trying to control other people's struggles.

The Lord calls us to stand in the gap of faith, to pray, and to serve others. If we know the Lord's freedom, then we are free to

love and encourage, not just serve our own egos. We can be led by our faith and God's providential plans to point people to the healer, Jesus. The Lord is so faithful and will bring people into our lives that encourage us and confirm His inner workings of healing. My friend Shellie sent me the above photo from one drop of her drink that fell on her napkin.

Just like that, in a moment with our King, He says, *I'm with you and for you.* Shellie is also an indie author and has been called to write about women aligning their hearts with Christ. We have walked together in faith, experiencing the goodness of God, not only for ourselves but within other women's hearts. We are all equal in the Father's eyes and in the stories that He is still writing.

PRAYER

Father, You are the author and finisher of my faith. Your goodness is running after me, every hour of every day. Bring the people into my life that will walk alongside me and encourage me on toward Your great works. You have already written the story of my life. Help me to find and accept the story and purpose You have for me, and to give You all the glory for it. In Jesus' name, amen.

ANOINTED
DAUGHTER

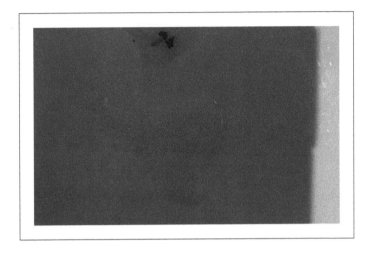

You have loved righteousness and hated wickedness.
Therefore God, your God, has anointed you with the oil
of gladness beyond your companions.
PSALM 45:7 ESV

The Lord's throne is forever. We are His daughters of royalty.
When we think of royalty, we think of powerful people, wealth,
status, regal character, nobility, royal lineage, or sovereignty.
These attributes are exactly what the Lord anoints us with when
we accept Him as our Father and become His daughters. It is not
to build ourselves up in our flesh, but to live in wholeness and to
serve those around us. Our God's kingdom is eternal, and so are
His ways. We were created to be loved by God and to love others
with that same love.

We are able to have complete joy, lacking nothing, in our Father's house. He is building a spiritual house here on earth, for all of eternity. Our redeemer redeems every area of our lives and removes what is not of Him. Whether it is learned behaviors, or areas of our hearts that are deceived, Jesus gave up His life so that we may have healing and wholeness here on earth, to be His royal priesthood. We cannot be a witness to the image of Christ if we are entangled in our own bondages, which pull us away from our Father's heart. When we love the way God loves, He anoints us with a joyful spirit, which enables us to walk in His commandments. Through obedience, the Lord's people gain all the attributes of the royal priesthood. My daughter, Loren, received this miracle heart, in olive oil, on Good Friday.

PRAYER

Heavenly Father, I am Your daughter and I turn my heart to receive Your joy and commandments that give me wholeness in Christ Jesus. Remove any wickedness from my heart and replace it with Your anointing, to fulfill the laws You have set on my heart. Thank You for redeeming me from the curse and weaving me into Your royal priesthood of believers. The joy of the Lord is my strength. In Jesus' name, amen.

PRESERVATION
FOR GENERATIONS

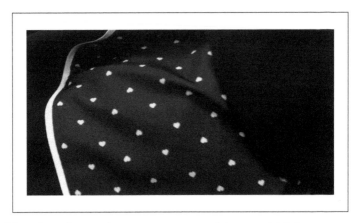

Therefore do not throw away your confidence, which has a great reward. For you have need of endurance, so that when you have done the will of God you may receive what is promised.

HEBREWS 10:35-36 ESV

God gave me and my brother, Cheth, a gift through our Aunt Diana and Uncle Mike, after my dad committed suicide when I was ten years old. They stepped into our lives in greater ways, to be an example to us and show us how to live, not just survive. Summers at their home was a reprieve for us from living in continual survival mode, due to abusive step-fathers. I know their goal was to be an example to all of their nephews and me, but I don't think they fully realized the impact they had on each of us. All God needs is a willing, yielded heart to serve, and He does miracles through it.

I cannot help but to see the threads of restoration that the Lord was doing through two people who did not grow up in healthy

homes themselves and were severely neglected. When we open our hearts to see God's provisions and grace in our lives, it compels us to want to pass that on, in the ways the Lord calls us to love others. Our experiences of God's grace aren't always wrapped up in a pretty little bow. Typically, His grace is shown through sacrificial love, by using people and situations that we could never imagine on our own.

My sweet uncle passed away last year, and at the funeral home, my aunt looked down to see hearts inside her jacket's lining. She always thought they were polka dots. God sees our pain and extends His love and grace. We all have loss in this world, but if we do not turn away from our Creator, He will show us great miracles and mercies. We will receive great rewards because we endured and did not throw away our confidence. When we do the will of God, His love is revealed to us in even greater ways.

PRAYER

Father, You are my gracious, loving Father. There is no pain or loss that heaven can't heal. Your love for me is all I need as I walk toward the paths You have called me. Show me Your promises and give me Your strength to endure so that I may receive all the benefits of doing Your will in my life. I love You. Thank You for Your love that has no end. In Jesus' name, amen.

MOMENTS WITH
THE KING

You keep him in perfect peace whose mind is stayed
on you, because he trusts in you. Trust in the Lord forever,
for the Lord God is an everlasting rock.

PROVERBS 16:24 ESV

It's not if, but when, we have troubles. Through having a relationship with Jesus and trusting in Him, we can keep our eyes on His word and heart He has for us. Then we may experience the supernatural works of the Lord. Circumstances and emotions change, but the word of God does not change. The above photo was taken as I was waiting for a call back for an MRI for a mammogram. This occurred the same week I was leaving for my uncle's funeral. There were several hearts during this week as well. However, I was at peace—but not happy—about getting called back again for another MRI. I saw someone from high school who was in the same boat as me, and I shared with her that I had just seen the heart and that God was with us.

I felt like the enemy was trying his best to attack me and get me to focus on the negative. The gift of the hearts was spoken to

me by God after my mom passed away from breast cancer. So, you can see where the enemy will want to use this moment to steal my peace and joy. The enemy's goal is to pull us away from faith and send us into doubt and fear. The Lord showed me the heart on the Post-it Note as I was checking in for my MRI.

I had to return, yet another day, for a biopsy, just to be sure. I will confess, I was very frustrated, and internally, I was mad that I had to go back. However, after praying continuously and keeping my thoughts on the Lord, as I was finishing up, the doctor told me she was all done, and the heart clip was in place. Apparently, when women have a breast biopsy, they put a sesame seed-sized clip in that spot. She chose the heart one for me out of fifteen different clips. I was in shock when she told me. The Lord quickly said to me, *I have you and you are Mine. Trust Me.* Praise God, my biopsy came back all clear.

PRAYER

Heavenly Father, give me eyes to see that, sometimes, You are calling me to walk through the unpleasantness in order to see Your faithfulness and to share it with others. I will not be moved, and my trust is in You, Jesus. Keep my mind on You and lead me in Your truths. You are my everlasting rock, and I praise You for divine health. In Jesus' name, amen.

REPENTANCE AND WALKING IN THE LIGHT

He stores up sound wisdom for the upright; he is a shield to those who walk in integrity, guarding the paths of justice and watching over the way of his saints. Then you will understand righteousness and justice and equity, every good path; for wisdom will come into your heart, and knowledge will be pleasant to your soul; discretion will watch over you, understanding will guard you, delivering you from the way of evil, from men of perverted speech, who forsake the paths of uprightness to walk in the ways of darkness, who rejoice in doing evil and delight in the perverseness of evil, men whose paths are crooked, and who are devious in their ways.

PROVERBS 2:7-15 ESV

The covering and provision God gives us through His word is miraculous. Our sacrifices are never in vain and never return void. Jesus was an exile for each one of us; will we be one for Him in return? Eternity is our home, and God's word shows us how to get there. When we receive Jesus into our hearts, we become children of the light and we should walk as children of the light. We are delivered from evil, and we are protected by the Lord's

shield when we repent. Repentance leads to the fruit of the Spirit, which is all goodness, righteousness, and truth. We are able to have the fruit of the Spirit, but we have a choice in how we will walk out in our faith. We should fear the Lord, more than we fear men.

My step-sister, Alecia, has walked in these promises. She has seen the powerful testimony and has witnessed God's miraculous presence and living word come to pass in her life. This apostrophe cloud was a gift to her when she came outside, after seeking God in a difficult situation. In our daily challenges, we can either turn away from or toward wisdom. We can either reap what the enemy's plans are for our lives or what God has already ordered before us. Stay the course, dwell in the land of the living, and reap the full benefits of God's promises and miraculous power here on earth, as it is in heaven.

PRAYER

Heavenly Father, I repent of every deed and thought that is not of the fruit of the Spirit. I choose Your wisdom and truth so that I may dwell in Your safety and have an understanding of righteousness and justice. Help me to keep my path straight and my heart far from darkness. In Jesus' name, amen.

A KINGDOM THAT
CANNOT BE SHAKEN

Therefore let us be grateful for receiving a kingdom that cannot
be shaken, and thus let us offer to God acceptable worship, with
reverence and awe, for our God is a consuming fire.

HEBREWS 12:28-29 ESV

All things in our lives can be shaken. I am sure that each of us has
many stories of loss and pain. The things and kingdoms of this
world are temporary, and the only lasting hope we have is Jesus
and His kingdom, which cannot be shaken. It is life to our souls
to know that we can receive lasting peace, joy, love, provision,
hope, favor, health, wisdom, and grace in every season of life
that we face. Jesus says that we can experience heaven on earth
because He brought it down to earth. If we will live sacrificially,

offering our praises to the one who is the King of our hearts, our hearts will be healed and kept by the blood of the Lamb.

Our hearts are meant to be lifted in worship to exalt our King. Jesus is the same yesterday, today, and forever. The Lord does not leave, nor forsake us. He will make our path straight in the plans He has for us, in building His unshakable kingdom on earth, set for all of eternity. Each of us may worship the Lord with gratitude and honor, in thanksgiving for sanctifying our stained hearts. The Holy Spirit is the only way to change our language to a heavenly language, and He enables us to have His fruit on our lips. The unshakable kingdom of Jesus extends goodness and love to all of us. Let us all reach to live honorable lives, pleasing to our Father in heaven.

PRAYER

Father, I praise You for Your unshakable kingdom and for the fruit of the Holy Spirit that gives me an eternal life and perspective. I pray that all of Your attributes rise up within me and pour out onto those around me. Break my heart for what breaks Yours, and guide me to complete every good work in Your will for me. In Jesus' name, amen.

LOVE ONE ANOTHER

Love one another with brotherly affection.
Outdo one another in showing honor.
ROMANS 12:10 ESV

It's easy to love the ones that love us. Jesus calls us to love people that are different from ourselves and people that may not return anything to us. Loving people in this way, and even having this ability, has to come from our spirits. We can't have love like this when we are focused on the things of the flesh. When we put our focus on the hearts of each man, we are looking at others with God's eyes. God's word teaches us how to love. We can keep our hearts focused on love when we love our enemies by praying for

DAY 85

them and not cursing them. The Holy Spirit does the miraculous in our hearts through fervent prayer.

Brotherly affection isn't about looking good or receiving a pat on the back in front of others because we have done a good thing. Freedom is giving love freely to people in our lives and expecting nothing in return. Our flesh wants accolades, but by outdoing one another in brotherly love, we are building an eternal legacy that builds bridges to heaven's purposes. When we learn how much we are loved by God, even though we don't deserve it, we may then love our neighbors as ourselves.

PRAYER

Heavenly Father, You laid down Your life for me when I was still a sinner and far from You. I want to love others in the same ways that You have loved me. Holy Spirit, give me Your eyes and strength to lead others in Your ways. Remove anything that is not of You from my heart. I give You all the honor and glory for the love I am able to share with others. In Jesus' name, amen.

MOVING THROUGH WITH THE HOLY SPIRIT

When you pass through the waters, I will be with you; and through the rivers, they shall not overwhelm you; when you walk through fire you shall not be burned, and the flame shall not consume you.

ISAIAH 43:2 ESV

When you walk through the fire, you will not be burned. Whether you are going through a fire you're in it now or if you have just come out on the other side, keep your eyes on Jesus. He will make all things new and bring us wholeness in every step. Have you ever been a caretaker, or met someone who is? Caretakers walk through fires all the time. My dear friend Dianne is a caretaker and a beautiful example of someone who trusts in God, taking one step at a time. She faithfully waits and leans on the Lord, even when she doesn't see immediate results. We don't need perfect execution; we need to learn how to trust, hold our peace, and listen to our Heavenly Father. She yields all of her emotions to the Father, and her words are kind and full of wisdom.

Our culture demands now and yesterday. But that is not how the things of heaven, or how the Holy Spirit, always operates. As we wait, we don't want to drift away from the Lord. We want to be built up in His truth and love. Our Father is much more concerned with how each of our hearts are joining His.

While I was listening to Dianne share an encouraging word to women that serve the Lord, the Lord said to me, "I will confirm it with a heart." To my surprise, as we were leaving, the above heart trivet was in our plain sight. The scripture in Isaiah says that we are precious in the Lord's eyes, honored, and loved. No matter what we face in this life, experiencing God's love and having it poured out over us is miraculous, and it is the sweetest love we will ever receive. Hebrews 2:4 teaches us, "God also bore witness by signs and wonders and various miracles and by gifts of the Holy Spirit distributed according to his will."

PRAYER

Heavenly Father, I set my sight on You. I can walk through my challenges, seeing Your miracles in my life, and not just seeing what I want, when I want it. You move mountains in my life every day. You raise my body to fullness, and You break every weight off of my heart. I will worship and honor You for all my days. Thank You for the gift of the Holy Spirit and Your never-ending affection. In Jesus' name, amen.

LOVE HAS A NAME

Anyone who does not love does
not know God, because God is love.

1 JOHN 4:8 ESV

God is love. Because of His love for us, He sent His one and only son, Jesus, so that we might learn how to love, just like the Father. First John teaches us not to believe every spirit. There are many false prophets in the world. Daughters, you will know the Spirit of God because every spirit of the Lord will confess that Jesus has come from God.

Every other spirit that does not confess this is of the antichrist. The battle on earth is spiritual, and it is for the hearts of man. God's glory is the only thing that enables us to be one with the Father and one with each other. We must be one first, and then celebrate all of our uniqueness. When she walked out onto her porch, my friend Shera found this hickory nut with a heart inside. God's love was reaching out to her heart and drawing her to love Him.

The book of John teaches us that Jesus gave us the glory so that we may be one, like Jesus is with God and the Holy Spirit. And that the world will know us as Jesus' by our unity. The glory is the manifest presence of the Holy Spirit. Jesus wants us to know the same love that He knows from God. In the presence of the Holy Spirit, there are no barriers or walls.

When we pray fervently together, in one accord, we preserve unity of the Spirit. The only way to have unity is through the Holy Spirit. We are equal when the Holy Spirit is poured out on all flesh, and there is no age, gender, or preferences to have or have nots. Refer to Acts 2:17-19 about the Holy Spirit at Pentecost. Jesus came to be our answer. We are found, and all of our needs are met in the ways of the kingdom, not the ways of this world.

PRAYER

Father, You are love, and I am grateful for Your love for me and for the ability to share Your love. Create in me a spirit that is pleasing to You. The value and honor You place on me and others reflect complete wholeness and unity by Your Holy Spirit. I gladly come to You in prayer daily, agreeing with Your word, for Your kingdom come and Your will be done on earth, as it is in heaven. In Jesus' name, amen.

WORSHIP
OVER WORRY

There is no fear in love, but perfect love casts out fear.
For fear has to do with punishment, and whoever fears
has not been perfected in love.

1 JOHN 4:18 ESV

We are chosen, not forgotten, as we are children of God. There is a place for each of us at the Lord's table of abundance, in everything our hearts long for, in perfect love. I don't know about you, but when I worship God through music, all fear, uncertainty, and worry is removed from my mind and heart. In the posture of humbling myself unto the Lord and holding up His truths above my emotions, He removes all fear. It is a space where often He reveals things to our hearts that need to be said and opens our eyes to the ways of our thinking that do not line up with His word. God tells us that He inhabits the praises of His people.

He meets us there. And when we cry out to God from the deep places of our souls, He answers.

During the global pandemic of 2020, I had so many heart photos sent to me in the first week of quarantine. God was with His people, blessing them with His love, presence, and peace while they celebrated birthdays, went on walks, had church in their homes, made meals, and spent time with their families in quarantine. Our source of life is found dwelling with God, and He is calling us to deeper places of security and wholeness in Him. God uses our struggles to draw us nearer to His heart, which helps us draw nearer to one another in His perfect love. If we will choose worship whenever worry comes, we may experience the refuge and inheritance of King Jesus, our Father.

PRAYER

Heavenly Father, worship is my weapon in the spirit realm. My fear is removed in Your perfect love. Break the lies, emotional strongholds, thoughts, and suggestions that are not from You. When I set my love on You, You deliver me and uphold me with Your righteous right hand. I can safely put my trust in You. In Jesus' name, amen.

NEW MERCIES
EVERY DAY

The steadfast love of the Lord never ceases; his mercies
never come to an end; they are new every morning; great
is your faithfulness. "The Lord is my portion," says
my soul, "therefore I will hope in him."
LAMENTATIONS 3:22-24 ESV

After seeing this heart on my table Christmas Eve morning,
I couldn't help but sing, *Great is thy faithfulness! Morning by
morning, new mercies I see.* The Father wants our hearts, and He
wants us to know His miraculous, consuming fire of a heart. The
holidays can be hard for those of us that have had parents or other
loved ones pass away. Christmas was my mom's favorite holiday.
I think of her often during this time because we have so many
memories around this holiday.

How gracious is the Lord to show us wonders of His love, especially when He knows we need it? God's love is the only thing that I have encountered that eases the sting of loss in this life. In these powerful moments of His mercies and compassion, we get to experience His steadfast love. We may move from sorrow to thanksgiving because of Jesus' pure, holy, righteous, and eternal love. His love breaks into the hard things in our lives when we are within His glorious presence. It is so comforting to know that His mercies have no end for us and that they are manifested in new ways and in every morning.

PRAYER

Heavenly Father, I am astounded by the way You love me and show me Your mercies every day. I receive Your mercies in my life, and I will put no one before You. I put my love and trust in You to carry all of my pain. I know that Your faithfulness will meet me. You are my portion that fills all of my needs. Thank You for Your unending mercies for me. In Jesus' name, amen.

HOPE UNTIL
THE VERY END

Although he was a son, he learned obedience through what he
suffered. . . . For God is not unjust so as to overlook your work
and the love that you have shown for his name in serving the saints,
as you still do. And we desire each one of you to show the same
earnestness to have the full assurance of hope until the end, so
that you may not be sluggish, but imitators of those who through
faith and patience inherit the promises.

HEBREWS 5:8 AND 6:10-12 ESV

We have a call to lay down the dead works in our lives through
repentance and to have faith toward God through the things we
suffer. Those that have tasted the heavenly gift of the Holy Spirit
and the goodness of God's word have moved toward a more
mature faith. However, we must stand firm in our assurance in
the Lord and imitate His ways so that we will inherit the Lord's
promises. It is only by God's glory that our weak flesh and spirit
are strengthened and our souls are refreshed. In this posture, God

DAY
90

gets our attention, and therefore, the things that we are putting before Him are removed, and order is restored in our hearts.

God still gives to us, even when things are being taken away. This exchange opens our eyes to God's ways, instead of our own ways. We choose to let His love invade our spaces so that we may be restored and be a part of His plans. We do not suffer in vain, but rather we have a hope and an anchor for our souls that is connected to eternity forever. Jesus wants us to be an example of His kingdom through the things we suffer. How incredible that God has set eternity in the heart of every man, as well as the mysteries of His unfolding of all things. He encourages us by teaching us that He has made everything beautiful in its time. We can't escape suffering. It is part of this fallen world, but it is such good news that, through it, we can produce much good fruit.

PRAYER

Father, it is through Your Spirit and obedience that I can stand firm, mature into wholeness, and receive Your promises. Jesus, You are my hope. I can lay hold of my inheritance through Christ Jesus and know blessings, even when things are taken away. Guide me toward all of Your plans for me. In Jesus' name, amen.

MARKED BY
LOVE FOR LOVE

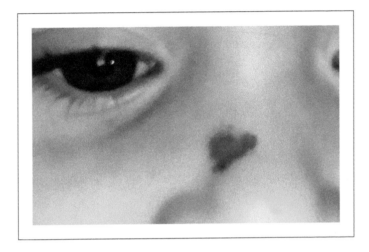

By this all people will know that you are my disciples,
if you have love for one another.

JOHN 13:35 ESV

We are all marked by the love of God, as His creation for love.
What a sweet gentle reminder for my friend Lisa and her family.
Her grandson had a scratch that turned into a heart as it healed.
When our focus is locked onto God's unconditional love, we can
have a clear vision that aligns with our Father in heaven. God
takes our blurred lens, which has been corrupted by the world,
and replaces it with His eyes. To live as Christ Jesus is to live with
eternal value, in wholeness and freedom and full of purpose. Jesus'
power and love, through a relationship with Him, is enough.

We can love one another because of Christ in us, when we receive Jesus into our hearts. God deserves all the glory and honor because He is the source of true love. Our Father in heaven never gets it wrong. He loves each of us so intimately and perfectly. When we, His disciples, quiet our own voices and lean in, listening to the ways the Father would have us love each other, miracles and mercies thrive. We live to please the Father, to have His truth and compassion shine through us. Jesus is our source of life, and all of His ways lead us to provision and to the still waters of His peace and love.

PRAYER

Heavenly Father, You mark me by Your love for love. Today, I will quiet my mind before You and listen, for the purposes of sharing Your love with those around me. I am a part of Your body and have a purpose in Your kingdom to love others. Let Your Holy Spirit fall on me, to guide me and empower me to complete all You have called me to do. In Jesus' name, amen.

SURRENDERED HEARTS

You shall love the Lord your God with all your heart
and with all your soul and with all your might. And these
words that I command you today shall be on your heart.
You shall teach them diligently to your children, and shall talk of
them when you sit in your house, and when you walk by the way,
and when you lie down, and when you rise.

DEUTERONOMY 6:5-7 ESV

God is looking for people with surrendered hearts that are on fire for Him. God is with us and for us, and His power and love is within us. He has shown His great love to us at every turn. The Lord calls His daughters to give Him their hearts and let their eyes delight in His ways. Let all that you do be done with love. Ephesians explains that the Lord gave prophets, teachers, and shepherds to equip the saints for the work of the ministry, for building up the body of Christ. So that we, as His royal priesthood, may mature into the fullness of Christ. We are not to be pulled to and from by every wind of doctrine, craftiness, and deceitful schemes.

DAY
92

Instead, every part of the body of Christ works properly, growing and being built up in love. We may bear with one another in love, maintaining the bond of unity and peace through humility, gentleness, and patience. We don't miss out on anything by having a surrendered heart. The Bible points us to sowing and reaping, and that whoever sows sparingly will also reap sparingly, and whoever sows bountifully will reap bountifully. God loves a cheerful giver and is able to make His grace shine upon us, giving us abundance, always, for every good work. Abundance in relationships, work, a peaceful spirit, and the supplying of our needs. When we receive the Lord's promise, let us not forget that it was not by our own merit, but from the hand of the Lord. It is because of the Lord that we serve and believe all things are possible.

PRAYER

Father, I am no longer a slave to the schemes of this world's system. I have abundance and freedom because of Your grace. It is by Your hand that I may know my place in the body of Christ. I humble myself and surrender to every good work You call to me for Your kingdom. All honor and glory to our King. In Jesus' name, amen.

GOD CONFIDENCE

The effect of righteousness will be peace, and the result of
righteousness, quietness and trust forever.

ISAIAH 32:17 ESV

There are many ways that God is speaking to us. He desires for
us to know Him so that we may have His confidence. Scripture
tells us that the Lord's invisible attributes, like His divine nature
and eternal power, are perceived clearly, since the creation of
the world. One of these ways has been through the hearts, but
God can speak through any method, such as wise counsel, other
people, dreams or visions, a whisper, supernaturally, the word of
God, the feeling of peace, and nature manifestations. Though we
must ask ourselves if are we listening. If we are listening to God,
then great, lasting faith is shown by acting on it with confidence.

We are not just the sum of what we do. We are the sum of Jesus' great love for us. When we encounter His love, it changes how we think about everything and, most important, how we think about ourselves. We find peace in seeking and seeing the Holy Spirit move. The Lord has used the hearts to manifest His consuming love for us, in the big and small moments, whether unbearable, glorious, mundane, important, joyful, or sad.

Jesus wants to be at the center of it all. We must lose our religion and experience a relationship with Jesus; it enables us to find out who He really is. We can be free from having to wear masks and living out a performance-based faith. This beautiful heart photo was from one of my daughter's friend's gardens. A caterpillar ate a hole into the shape of a heart. What a beautiful way for the Lord to delight in His daughter.

PRAYER

Heavenly Father, Your grace and mercy chases me down, to raise me up in Your confidence and peace. I want to hear You and see You leading me to places of security while in Your presence. I want to make You the center of my life, in all of the changing circumstances of my day. Give me ears to hear and eyes to see Your favor and blessings in my life. In Jesus' name, amen.

WONDERS ARE STILL WHAT YOU DO

With man this is impossible, but with God all things are possible.

MATTHEW 19:26 ESV

Loving our neighbor as ourselves may seem impossible. Not everyone is easy to love. But the impossible is made possible when we set our hearts on God. We must be connected to the source of pure righteousness in order to have a heart on fire for the ways of God. When our sight is on Jesus and we worship Him and set our hearts on Him, watch what He does. It seems so simple, and it really is. We have so much intellectual information that surrounds us daily, making it easy to be self-reliant and drift from the simple truth that God is the source of our intellect and wisdom. Eternal wisdom and knowledge may only be attained by pressing into sacred time spent with our Creator. Then, we may have eyes to see His wonders.

Wonders and miracles happen when the Lord moves. The only way we will see Him move is by knowing Him and being

surrendered to Him. Our Lord is all of the good that is in us. When we are self-centered and take all the credit, we begin to miss the glory and wonder of our King. God meant for us to experience His kingdom here on earth by being the expressions of His love and wisdom for all people.

As we set our sights and minds on our King, He moves mountains, raises bodies to their fullness, and gives each of us a clear vision. The most beautiful, breathtaking thing to witness is God's love and wonder. As we pursue the kingdom's attributes, everything else will be added to us. Proverbs instructs us that whoever pursues righteousness and love will find prosperity, life, and honor.

PRAYER

Heavenly Father, I will pursue righteousness and love in all that I do. I set my heart on You and wait on the Lord for all of the wonders and miracles You faithfully pour out. Thank You for healing my heart as I live my life for You. Show me the ways that You would have me extend the kingdom to those around me today—whether it is through forgiveness or serving in any way that You are calling me to give of myself, for the building up of those around me. I give You all the praise for making the impossible things in my life possible. In Jesus' name, amen.

THE GLORY
OF GOD

My dwelling place shall be with them,
and I will be their God, and they shall be my people.

EZEKIEL 37:27 ESV

We must place our reliance on God's word, not our own words.
It is only God's power that will bless men and bring their hearts
back to life. God's word has supernatural power. God's glory
and Spirit is what gives our dry bones and fractured hearts life
again. We may receive restoration and regain our breath back to
places of wholeness because of the Holy Spirit. The Lord's new
covenant with His people is shalom, or peace, for here on earth.
He is calling His people out of sin and from having other idols
put before God, to come together in unity and be restored.

The world will know God's people by the restoration of His
sanctuary here on earth, in the midst of wars and wickedness. We,

as individuals, are the temple of God, dwelling in the land as a beacon of purity and devotion to King Jesus. Ezekiel 43 describes the glory of God as nothing more than extraordinary. Visually, he saw God's glory coming from the east, shining upon the whole earth and sounding like many waters.

Like Israel, we may become used to God's magnificent glory, where it becomes common in our minds. But when we repent and reestablish and connect back in relationship with God, we again experience the blessing of His presence and glory! God has set His presence among His people. He is always in pursuit of our hearts and minds, and when we set our hearts on God, His presence is there. God is a God of order, and He wants our loyalty. We just have to create that space for connection.

PRAYER

Father, thank You for the glory of God in my life. I am loyal to You, King Jesus. I want to know Your love for me and see Your hand and breath moving in my life. Thank You for Your glory that brings unity in Your people. I will preserve the unity of the spirit by keeping my loyalty to Jesus above all other things. I pray Your shalom over my life, in the midst of all that I face day to day. In Jesus' name, amen.

CONTENTMENT
IN GOD'S LOVE

I can do all things through him who strengthens me.
PHILIPPIANS 4:13 ESV

We have all been brought low, abounding in the circumstances of life. Suffering is what brings us together and gives us the ability to relate to each other, regardless of our exterior differences. The enemy wants us to believe that we are all alone in our season of pain and suffering. But when we know the Holy Spirit and have learned the secret to be content in every circumstance, either plenteous or in need, we gain strength through Christ. We may rise each day in our lives and meet with our God, who enlightens and refreshes us to carry our cross. We may know that God will supply every need that we have, according to His riches, in glory in Christ Jesus.

Scripture doesn't say some of our needs; it says all of our needs. As Christ followers, we are called to share in our troubles and to praise God through the benefits of His supernatural word. After

learning about the heart story, my dear friend Beverly noticed this heart that she gave her husband decades ago, having always hung on his wardrobe. God used it to minister to her in that moment as her husband was battling a disease.

They have been married for over fifty years and have faithfully served the Lord during their marriage. Through her moments with the King, in seeing hearts and rainbows, God spoke to her that God needed to be first in her heart, even before her husband. God knew that she needed His strength and presence in greater depth before she would have her mother and husband pass away within a year of one another. How gracious and faithful is our God. Our strength comes from the Lord, and the more faithful we are in seeking out our King and putting Him first in our hearts, the more contentment and wholeness He will pour out into our hearts in every moment of every season.

PRAYER

Heavenly Father, I can do all things through Christ who strengthens me. I will put You first and meet You in the morning, throughout my day, and in the evening, to receive Your supernatural love and wisdom that gives me everything I need in every circumstance. You are my first love and are everything to me. In Jesus' name, amen.

MY REFUGE
AND FORTRESS

Because you have made the Lord your dwelling place—the Most High,
who is my refuge—no evil shall be allowed to befall you, no plague
come near your tent. For he will command his angels concerning you
to guard you in all your ways. On their hands they will bear you up,
lest you strike your foot against a stone. You will tread on the lion and
the adder [cobra]; the young lion and the serpent you will trample
underfoot. "Because he holds fast to me in love, I will deliver him; I will
protect him, because he knows my name. When he calls to me, I will
answer him; I will be with him in trouble; I will rescue him and honor
him. With long life I will satisfy him and show him my salvation."

PSALM 91:9-16 ESV

What if we lived our lives daily around the fact that God's love
surrounds us? What if we have the awareness of God's love
working on our behalf, in every little detail of our days? God
extends His refuge and safe place of protection for those that
love Him. It is quite miraculous and life-changing to have this
wisdom and understanding of our Creator. I think, sometimes,
it is difficult for us to realize this because of the limitations and

busyness of our minds. The heart encounters give us joy and strength in the midst of our overwhelming days. God blesses us with His love and presence in a multitude of ways.

As I am writing this devotional, our country is in the throngs of a pandemic. Many people are experiencing peace in the middle of this difficult time through moments with our King and through the hearts. Quarantine has turned into extra quality time with the Lord, and our vision is being opened up to the workings of the Lord through loss and isolation. We may rest assured God is with us, and He is calling us to deeper places of security and wholeness in Him. As we draw nearer to our Father's heart, it enables us to better draw nearer to one another in His perfect love.

PRAYER

Heavenly Father, You are my fortress and safe place. I will cling to You and trust in Your love for me. I know that my Father in heaven works all things together for my good. Thank You that no evil will befall on me, neither plague near my dwelling. I pray for Your hedge of protection over me and my loved ones every day. I praise You that I can be the head, and not the tail, and anything that is not of You is under my feet and defeated. In Jesus' name, amen.

WORSHIP AND REMEMBRANCE

Now as they were eating, Jesus took bread, and after blessing it broke it and gave it to the disciples, and said, "Take, eat; this is my body." And he took a cup, and when he had given thanks he gave it to them, saying, "Drink of it, all of you, for this is my blood of the covenant, which is poured out for many for the forgiveness of sins."

MATTHEW 26:26-28 ESV

Communion began on Passover, the day Jesus told his disciples to remember His sacrifice. The Israelites celebrated the Passover lamb when the death angel passed over their homes. Believers today celebrate and remember the ultimate Passover Lamb, Jesus, who was sacrificed and crucified on the cross for our sins. The bread symbolizes Jesus' body that was broken for our sins and the wine represents Jesus' blood that forgives us of all of our sins. God has given us a new covenant in Jesus. Communion brings us to

DAY 98

the table of the Lord, where we worship and remember Jesus and are made whole.

My friend Hannah's son took a bite of his communion cracker on Passover to see this heart. Jesus is God, who is with us and for us. Communion is sacred and such a powerful representation of God calling us to Jesus. By Jesus being put to death in His body, He was able to be made fully alive in the Spirit. It is the same for the children of God.

When we receive Jesus into our hearts, we are made alive in our spirits, and the Lord's bread from heaven gives us life. Each of us should examine our own hearts before we eat the bread and take from the cup. We want to discern our hearts and be alert to the health of it. We are healed and continuously made whole through this yielding and surrendering to what the Holy Spirit is revealing to each of His daughters.

PRAYER

Heavenly Father, I worship You through communion and give thanks for Your sacrifice for me, and for all of my sins being forgiven. Search my heart and show me things that are not of You. Reveal Your truths to me so that I may be free to love like You. In Jesus' name, amen.

LET LOVE LEAD

If I speak in the tongues of men and of angels, but have not love,
I am a noisy gong or a clanging cymbal. And if I have prophetic
powers, and understand all mysteries and all knowledge, and if I
have all faith, so as to remove mountains, but have not love, I am
nothing. If I give away all I have, and if I deliver up my body to be
burned, but have not love, I gain nothing. Love is patient and kind;
love does not envy or boast; it is not arrogant or rude. It does not
insist on its own way; it is not irritable or resentful; it does not
rejoice at wrongdoing, but rejoices with the truth. Love bears all
things, believes all things, hopes all things, endures all things.

1 CORINTHIANS 13:1-7 ESV

I would like to linger on this scripture. If we take the time to
really listen to this scripture as a Jesus-follower, we are truly made
aware of how important love is to God. We may have all of these
different gifts from the Lord, but if we don't use them with love
as the lead, we miss it completely and are not productive for the
kingdom. With knowledge comes power. But in Christ, He is

our power, which He expresses through His love. This scripture can bring us back to the greatest of all good, which is love. Love in Christ is where our healing begins and our freedom is found.

We can be whole in Christ, but not in what we accomplish or learn. God is always right on time. We may share His love in all that we do. The book of Romans tells us to not be overcome by evil, but to overcome evil with good. We are able to be a light in the darkness because of the light of Jesus in us, and the darkness cannot overcome it. Jesus is our light of life, and those of us that choose to walk in that light will never be overcome by the darkness. We may have hope in all things.

PRAYER

Heavenly Father, You are the light of the world, and You have given me gifts for Your kingdom purposes. Help me to see today the assignments that You have given me, to show Your love to others, and to give them hope and a future. In Jesus' name, amen.

PERFECT
PEACE

You keep him in perfect peace whose mind is
stayed on you, because he trusts in you.

ISAIAH 26:3 ESV

It is so true that if we can fix our thoughts, we may change our
lives. The gift of seeing hearts at God's providential timing is
a wonderful example of fixing our thoughts on Him, instead of
all the things in our lives that steal our joy and hope. He keeps
our minds fixed on Him, and through that devotion, the Lord
gives us His peace as we trust in Him. We can change the entire
trajectory of our lives by aligning our hearts with God's and by
receiving His unmerited favor and wisdom. When we open our
hearts to receive God's eternal love, we may truly be made whole
here on earth. We may make the most of our time here, for impact
in eternity.

Every single person on earth has a role to play and is a part of the body of Christ when they receive Jesus into their hearts. There are no leftovers or mistakes. God gives us, though, the dignity of choice. We have a choice to make, each day, who we will serve, whether man or God. We are made in the image of Christ, for a specific time and place, to be His image bearers.

The path of the righteous is made straight and level. Things come into focus when our thoughts are fixed on God. God fixes our thoughts. Everything else is a distraction. We must stay the course of heaven and dwell in God's perfect peace, to be able to receive God's royal love that makes us whole, healed, and free to love.

PRAYER

Heavenly Father, thank You for Your perfect peace that overcomes me when my heart is set on You. Holy Spirit, have Your way within me. Fan the flame of Your love within me. You are the King of my heart, and I praise You for all You have done within me, to give me Your peace, wisdom, and love. You hold me together in Your love. In Jesus' name, amen.

♥

SPECIAL THANKS

Thank You, God, for Your message of love in the hearts that ministers to so many people, helping each of us to return to our first love. I would like to give a special thanks to my family and friends who have encouraged me during the process of writing and telling God's stories. It has been beautiful and inspiring to see the love of God shine on everyone that has heart photos and stories, both in *A Royal Love Devotional* and beyond. Your willingness to share your testimonies and be vulnerable is a blessing to everyone around you. My editor, Kimberly Smith Ashley, I thank you for always saying just the right thing and for being a wealth of knowledge. My graphic designer, Summer Morris, so beautifully created the book's layout. To all of our friends and family who have been encouraged by God's love dipping down into these heart moments with King Jesus, we will never be the same. I am grateful to live this life with each of you, with kingdom purpose.

For this reason I bow my knees before the Father, from whom
every family in heaven and on earth is named, that according to the riches
of his glory he may grant you to be strengthened with power through his
Spirit in your inner being, so that Christ may dwell in your hearts through
faith—that you, being rooted and grounded in love, may have strength to
comprehend with all the saints what is the breadth and length and height
and depth, and to know the love of Christ that surpasses knowledge, that
you may be filled with all the fullness of God.

EPHESIANS 3:14-19 ESV

The Lord bless you, protect you, sustain you, and guard you; The Lord make His face shine upon you with favor, and be gracious to you, surrounding you with loving kindness; The Lord lift up His face upon you with divine approval, and give you a [peaceful] heart and life.

NUMBERS 6:24-26 AMP

ABOUT THE AUTHOR

Corrine Sharpe is an award-winning author of *A Royal Love Revealed: My Journey from Sorrow to God's Heart.* In addition to writing, she has led and been involved in countless women's Bible studies and community outreaches through her church, Celebration, for over nineteen years. She enjoys documenting her, and the many others', heart encounters that bring peace and hope in Jesus. She holds a bachelor's degree in Human and Health Performance from the University of Florida and lives in Florida with her husband and two children.

CONNECT WITH CORRINE AT CORRINESHARPE.COM

f **Instagram** **@CORRINESHARPE**